From Slaves to Oil

From Slaves to Oil

United States role in the plunder of Africa

DAVID MODEL

authorHOUSE®

AuthorHouse™ LLC
1663 Liberty Drive
Bloomington, IN 47403
www.authorhouse.com
Phone: 1-800-839-8640

Published by AuthorHouse 06/17/2014

ISBN: 978-1-4969-1982-3 (sc)
ISBN: 978-1-4969-1981-6 (e)

CONTENTS

DEDICATION

To my grandson Aidan, 2 ½ years old, for having the wisdom to be born in Canada, a country with a high standard of living and which is safe and secure.

INTRODUCTION

It is lavishly wealthy continent; it is devastatingly poor continent. Africa has always been far richer than Europe in resources but lagged light years behind in economic, industrial, social, military and political development. Despite its extreme wealth in resources such as gold, diamonds, ivory, oil, uranium, coltan, cobalt and rubber, Africa has been unable to capitalize on these advantages to promote any substantial progress in achieving stability or raising the standard of living of its peoples.

To account for this paradox, it is necessary to examine the relationship between Africa and the rest of the world. The greater European advancement in military prowess, political organization and, in particular, strong naval capabilities, in conjunction with the greed permeating European economic zeitgeist empowered first Europe then America to exploit the continent for cheap or free labor, bases, allies, markets and resources.

American and European dominance and exploitation of African countries, after they gained independence, is best understood in the context of post-colonial analysis. Post-colonialism is a hotly debated concept involving many fields of study but I will restrict myself to a definition formulated by Noam Chomsky who stated that: "The former imperial powers have laboured to ensure that the structures of power and exploitation remain largely in place [after independence]." In particular, Chomsky claims that Washington was determined to ensure that traditional structures of power with which the United States has long been aligned remain in power so that exploitation would meet with minimal resistance.

Post-colonialism required that friendly governments ruled in targeted countries. The United States resorted to a number of different strategies to secure subservient governments in power in victimized countries to ensure that its policies were favorable to the United States and its resources were readily available.

For example, some of the leaders who were not friendly were assassinated such as Trujillos in Panama in 1981, Roldos in Ecuador in 1981, Lumumba in the Congo in 1960, Allende in Chile in 1973.

Some were removed from power through the use of a proxy force including Ortega in Nicaragua in 1990 - the proxy was the Contras; Arbenz in Guatemala in 1954 - the proxy were ex-national guardsmen; Isabel Peron in Argentina in 1976 - the proxy were military leaders; the government of East Timor 1975 - the proxy was Suharto of Indonesia; Manly in Jamaica 1979 - the proxy was the World bank; and the Islamic government in Somalia - the proxy was the Ethiopian army. Others were removed from power by the CIA as was the case with Mossadegh in Iran in 1953 and Diem in Vietnam in 1963. In other words, either a leader supported American post-colonial policies or he/she was replaced.

When a government was identified as U.S.-friendly, Washington offered considerable support, mostly military, to secure that government in power. Maintaining brutal and corrupt dictators was the upshot of this policy. For example, the following is a sample of the brutal dictators who were supported by the United States:

* Iran - Shah of Iran, 1953 – 1979

* Guatemala – military dictators, 1954-1996

* Brazil - Military dictator, 1964-1985

* Congo – General Mobutu, 1965-1997

* Honduras military dictators, 1963 – 1980

* Argentina – military junta, 1976-1983

* Iraq – Saddam Hussein, 1979 – 1990

* Libya - Gaddafi, 1979 – 2003

* Egypt - Mubarak, 1981 – 2011

* Persian Gulf States, Royal Family, 1980 – present

* Chile - Pinochet, 1973 – 1990

* Panama – Noriega, 1982 – 1989

* Rwanda – Paul Kagame, 1994 to present

* Uganda – Museveni, 1986 – present

* Philippines – Marcos, 1965 – 1986

* Vietnam – Diem, 1955 – 1963

* Indonesia – Suharto, 1967 – 1998

* Cambodia – Lon Nol, 1970 - 1975

Perhaps the most salient example of this exploitation occurred in the Congo around the turn of the twentieth century. Between five and fifteen million people died in the Congo simply to aggrandize the personal wealth of King Leopold II of Belgium.

Leopold succeeded his father to the Belgium throne on December 17, 1865 and remained on the throne until his death on December 17, 1909. After a number of attempts to establish colonies in Africa, he created the International African Society (IAS) in 1876, a private holding company whose ostensible purpose was to promote scientific and philanthropic endeavors.

Its real purpose became evident when Leopold, through the IAS, commissioned the famous explorer Henry Morton Stanley, well-known for unearthing the whereabouts of Dr. Livingstone, to establish a colony in Africa. Following his initial instructions to construct a wagon trail and a series of forts and trading stations, he was ordered to carve out a new nation in Central Africa. Stanley signed treaties with over 400 African chiefs in which they abdicated sovereignty over their territory where Stanley established a network of outposts.

At the Berlin Conference of 1885, called for the purpose of dividing all African territories into colonies for the fourteen European nations in attendance, the land claimed by Leopold, known as the Congo Free State, was allocated to the IAS thereby securing Leopold's control over a huge part of Africa.

Leopold's primary ambition was to enrich himself by first collecting ivory through such ruthless methods as raiding villages, sending out hunting expeditions and whipping inhabitants who failed to cooperate. Ivory did not yield the riches he had expected and, as a result, he turned his attention to rubber.

The first rubber tires appeared in the mid-1850s. Rubber tires adoption for use on automobiles was pioneered by the Michelin brothers who equipped a car with pneumatic tires for the 1895 Paris-Bordeaux road race. In 1898, the Goodyear Tire and Rubber Company was formed followed by the founding of the Firestone Tire

& Rubber Company in 1900. Suddenly, the demand for rubber was increasing exponentially.

A growing demand for bicycles followed by cars drove up the price of rubber rapidly which engendered the potential for huge riches. As a result, King Leopold restricted foreign access to rubber trees and forced the local population into slave labor to work on the King's rubber farms in his new colony.

Leopold's methods for maintaining a system of slave labor and controlling the population were brutal and included savage beatings, imprisonment, widespread killing and setting daily quotas for each worker who risked the loss of their hands if they failed to meet it.

His methods greatly expanded the production of rubber from 100 tons of rubber in 1890 to 6000 tons in 1891. Another result of his methods were uprisings, revolts, burned villages, refugees, starvation and disease.

King Leopold's exploitation and human rights transgressions were the modality for advanced nation's relationships with Africa. An excellent framework for understanding this relationship is World Systems Theory which divides the world into periphery, semi-periphery and core countries. Core countries are characterized by high skill labor, capital-intensive production while peripheral countries are characterized by low-skill, labour-intensive countries. The core countries draw their resources from the peripheral countries and tend to control their development thus maintaining a system of inequality.

World Systems Theory is partially based on dependency theory where the core countries penetrate the peripheral countries for the purpose of exploitation, limiting self-sustained growth in the peripheral countries and breeding vast economic inequality reducing the peripheral countries to the status of "hewers of wood and drawers of water".

In order to exploit and violate the human rights of the peripheral countries, the core countries had to dehumanize the populations of these countries. Although a misinterpretation, Rudyard Kipling's "White Man's Burden" seemed to reinforce legitimization of imperial powers' brutal exploitation of Africa. The unconscionable villainy inflicted on the peoples of the "Dark Continent" underwent a number of phases which include the original scramble for territory and the concomitant atrocities, struggles for independence followed by post-colonial exploitation in which the United States has played a major role.

Since the sixteenth century when Portugal established permanent settlements along the coasts of Africa to the present day, Europe and the United States constructed a concept similar to that of Edward Said's "Orientalism" but applied to Africa, to justify plundering, massacres and looting of the continent's myriad resources desperately needed to fuel the industrial revolution and the age of technology.

By perceiving the African people as the "other", colonizers treated them in a somewhat similar fashion as the treatment of the natives in North America who were considered uncivilized, primitive and most importantly, inferior and superfluous. The land on which they lived was merely an inconvenience to the pioneers moving West who simply "took it"; the very same words used by Theodore Roosevelt when asked to explain his justification for taking the Panama Canal.

Murder and forced marches westward were some of the strategies employed to remove the natives from the land that clearly belonged to the colonizers, at least according to the colonizers. Twelve million Native Americans or 97% died during the colonization of the territory now referred to as the United States.

Another example relates to South America. Columbus is known for his voyage to America in 1492 but his real legacy was the slaughter of the vast majority of natives in the Caribbean. In 1493, Columbus returned to the New World with an invasion force of seventeen ships to conquer the inhabitants already there and to steal their wealth. Upon arrival, he declared himself governor and viceroy of the Caribbean islands and settled on the island of Española, now known as Haiti and the Dominican Republic.

Any obstacle posed by the native Taino population, who already occupied the land in the Caribbean, was quickly overcome through displacement, enslavement, and extermination. They were forced to abandon their well cultivated fields to work as slave labourers for their conquerors. As well, all Taino natives over the age of 14 were required to produce a hawk's bell of gold for the Spaniards or lose both their hands. Extermination assumed many shocking forms, including burning at the stake, hacking children into pieces for dog food and hanging or roasting on spits.

When Columbus first arrived in the Caribbean, there were about eight million inhabitants, but when he departed in 1500, his brutality and savagery had reduced their numbers to approximately 100,000. He had virtually annihilated the entire Taino population, setting a model for future explorers who were encumbered by local native populations.

The people of Africa were similarly an obstacle to the expansion, enrichment and prestige of the imperial powers of Europe and the United States. Given the history of brutality for the purpose of exploitation, it is not in the least surprising that Europeans and Americans would eradicate any barrier to their own enrichment and expansion in Africa.

During the industrial revolution, Imperial powers had developed weapons far superior to those in Africa thus providing the mechanism by which they could easily suppress any resistance to their grand designs.

Additionally, European countries had been at war with each other 206 times between 1500 and 1900. Some of the better known wars include the War of the Roses 1455-1466, Austrian-Hungarian war 1477-1488, Ottoman-Hapsburg War 1521-1718, Eighty Years War 1568-1648, Anglo-Spanish War 1585-1604, Thirty Years War 1616-1648, Napoleonic Wars 1803-1815 and Franco-Prussian War 1870-1871. During these wars, European nations had an opportunity to strengthen their armies, navies and weapons and were capable of completely overpowering any army in Africa with very few exceptions.

European countries scrambled for territory to purloin resources, force the locals to engage in slave labour, and to establish outposts for their empires. In the process, they deprived these nations of riches that rightly belonged to them and perpetrated the most heinous crimes against humanity in order to aggrandize their own wealth.

To regulate the fierce competition for colonies in Africa, Portugal called for a conference in Berlin in 1884 which was organized by Otto von Bismarck. The 1885 Berlin Conference crafted a set of rules to guide colonization in Africa. One of the rules determined which regions each European power had an exclusive right to and another prohibited the establishment of a colony in name only. By the end of the nineteenth century, Europe controlled all of the territory in Africa except Ethiopia and Liberia.

Despite efforts to regulate the plundering of Africa, a series of crises eventually capitulated Europe into World War 1 when previous rivalries and alliances divided Europe into two opposing sides who slaughtered each other in the bloody trenches of Europe to settle their imperialistic conflicts.

Prior to the independence of African nations, most European nations capitalized on the aforementioned advantages to pillage resources or expand their empires.

A number of examples elucidate the relations between Europe and Africa prior to independence.

According to the 1985 United Nations Whitaker Report, Germany was guilty of genocide in South-West Africa when it murdered 65,000 Herero and 10,000 Namaqua between 1904 and 1907 in an attempt to supress an uprising against German rule. The rebellion was quashed by 1908 and the inhabitants were subject to slave labour and a system of apartheid.

During the latter half of the nineteenth century, the British were preoccupied with consolidating their colonies in South Africa and securing access to their valuable resources, particularly diamonds. Their primary obstacle was the Zulu Kingdom with its standing army of 40,000 disciplined warriors. In January, 1879, the British were caught off guard and were defeated in the first Zulu war but with reinforcements, the British rebounded to defeat the Zulus in August of the same year. Crushing the Zulus was a critical point in South African history since the Zulus were the only power in the region that were capable of resisting white expansion.

Another example of British Imperialism took place when fifty British and French ships arrived in Alexandria Egypt in 1882 fomenting riots in Alexandria in which 50 Europeans were killed. Britain responded by ordering the British fleet to bombard Alexandria which destroyed most of the city following which British marines occupied the city. British occupation didn't end until 1936.

There is disagreement about the British motivations for their actions in Egypt which ran the gamut from preserving British control of the Suez Canal to protecting British investors who had financed the Canal.

In addition to Egypt, the UK decided that to maintain stability in the region and safeguard Egypt from the Mahdi forces in Sudan who were in control of most of the country, Mahdi forces would have to be crushed. British and Egyptian forces had already experienced defeat at the hands of the Mahdis, when the British/Egyptian forces attempted to rescue General Gordon in Khartoum in 1885.

In 1898, Horatio Herbert Kitchener led a 9,000 strong force into Sudan and defeated the Mahdist forces in the Battle of Atbara with the use of British machine guns and rifle power, killing 30,000. British control of the Sudan survived until its independence in 1956.

In retaliation for losses suffered during its first invasion of Ethiopia in 1896, Italy perpetrated monstrous crimes against humanity in Ethiopia from 1935 to 1936 by invading the country with 100,000 troops and 250 planes equipped with mustard gas. Villages, livestock and water sources were subject to the effects of the suffocating gas.

After Ethiopia surrendered, Marshall Rodolfo Graziani subjected the people to military occupation and a reign of terror in which a total of 760,000 people were killed.

After World War II, American foreign policy proposed securing control of the "Grand Area" which now extends to Africa, expedited by the creation of AFRICOM, construction of military bases, drone launching pads, and the establishment of allies and surrogates who serve as an arm of America's defense and foreign policy communities.

When African colonies gained independence they had no protection from the plundering and atrocities driven by European and American greed.

Chapter one examines the most horrendous human rights tragedy since World War II. Five to six million people died in the Congo since independence in 1960 from disease, war and starvation as a number of countries including the United States plundered the riches mostly located in the eastern part of the country. Ultimately, coltan, an ingredient essential to the manufacture of electronic chips for cell phones, blackberries and similar products became the coveted prize due to cheap labor given that many of the mine workers were young children.

Militias, proxy armies acting on behalf of the United States and the army of a brutal dictatorship roamed the country pillaging, raping and murdering the local inhabitants who were often forced to seek refuge in the jungle where food or clean water were virtually non-existent.

American complicity began with the overthrow of the first democratic government in the Congo immediately after independence which was then replaced with a brutal dictator who was supported by the United States along with his successors well into the 21 century.

Chapter two involves the support for a corrupt and brutal dictator in Somalia who was an ally to Washington. After the dictator was forced from power due to corruption and brutality, there was an absence of a central government for many years. When a leader opposed by the U.S. was threatening to form a government, an ostensible peace-keeping mission led by the U.S. turned into a disaster when the Americans launched an assault on Mogadishu, the capital, and ended up in an inglorious defeat known as "Black Hawk Down".

When a popular, moderate Islamic party formed the government, Washington commissioned Ethiopia to act as a proxy and invade Somalia. The doubly tragic impact of the invasion was the installation of an incompetent government supported by the United States and an insurgency determined to regain power for the Islamic party. Somalia was also flooded with weapons from Western countries creating one of the most dangerous countries in which to live.

Chapter three is an interesting case due to the fact that Libya was a fluctuating ally of the U.S. and Europe. At one point, Gaddafi transformed his economic system into one that was acceptable to the West. When Gaddafi began to defy the U.S., Libya became a potential target for American intervention.

Finally, in 2011 U.S and NATO attacked Libya under the guise of a humanitarian intervention to conceal the real motivation which was to overthrow Gaddafi and replace him with an American-friendly government. The leaders during the pseudo-insurgency were mostly trained and educated in the United States and had lived there for many years before they led the uprising and the newly formed government.

Libya had the highest United Nations Development Index in Africa before Western interference but is now in a state of chaos.

Chapter four discusses the fact that Ethiopia was acting as a proxy for Washington while at the same time committing genocide against Somalis living in the Ogaden region of Ethiopia. When Europe carved up Africa, it also divided the Somali people into many different countries including the Ogaden region. Somalis in these other countries were eager to become part of Somalia leading to a number of wars between Ethiopia and Somalia over who was going to gain possession of the Ogaden region.

As a means of ending the dispute, Ethiopia decided to exterminate the Somalis inside their borders.

Chapter five examines Rwanda where interest was piqued for several reasons. In order to establish a pro-U.S. government in Rwanda to serve as an ally and proxy, the U.S. became entangled in the civil war and genocide. An invading Tutsi army based in Uganda and led by Paul Kagame, was committed to overthrowing the Hutu government in Mogadishu.

Washington took the side of the invading Tutsi force during the civil war due to the expectation of support from their leader if they won.

As well, to avoid a Hutu victory in the civil war the U.S. deliberately stalled the deployment of a U.N. peacekeeping force that would have been capable of putting an end to the eventual slaughter of 800,000 Tutsis and moderate Hutus. Peace would probably have resulted in a coalition government whereas the U.S. wanted a Tutsi government that it could count on for support. The delaying tactics of President Clinton makes him complicit in the genocide.

Once the Tutsis were in power, the U.S. supported Rwanda's invasion of the Congo for the purpose of stealing resources. The flight of Tutsi's and Hutu's escaping the genocide and the extreme Hutu's escaping the post-genocidal government became another factor in the destruction of the Congo.

Also in chapter five, there is an examination of the genocide committed by LRA and President Museveni's army in Uganda against the Acholi people in Northern Uganda. American used Uganda as an extension of American military prowess to fight battles for the United States especially in Central Africa. Museveni, the president from 1986 to the present, has proven to be an invaluable ally who was willing to cooperate with American foreign policy initiatives anywhere in Africa.

Chapter six is an interesting case in as much as it serves as an example of the fate of a developing country cursed with an abundance of oil. Dutch and American oil companies began to search for oil in Nigeria and then construct the infrastructure and facilities to produce oil without the slightest regard for the people living on the land where the oil was located.

Human rights violations and destruction of the environment and the local people's way of life did not matter one iota to Shell, Chevron and the other oil companies operating in Nigeria.

The American government cooperated with the Nigerian government in providing security for the oil companies who were confronted with protests and riots. Shell and Chevron themselves assisted in their own security, in particular, by providing military equipment and arms to the Nigerian army and security forces.

Chapter seven discusses the strategic and economic importance of Liberia. As a result of its value, a number of brutal dictators received generous support from the United States only to ensure a friendly leader who would serve the interests of the United States. The United States supported Sam Doe in the 1980s and from 1997 to 2003 supported a leader, Charles Taylor, who was not only bent on becoming the president in Liberia but extending his power over Sierra Leone and other surrounding countries as well.

Charles Taylor fought the Liberian government for many years before becoming president in 1997 ending many years of civil war. His ambitions extended beyond Liberia and he was particularly interested in Sierra Leone. He created a militia known as the Revolutionary United Front (RUF) who recruited child soldiers and transformed them into psychotic killers. They fought for control of Sierra Leone.

Thucydides, Greek historian in the fifth century B.C.E., best summarized the plight of people in developing countries who suffer exploitation and human rights abuses at the hands of more powerful countries when he propounded the precocious insight that:

> As the world goes, right is only in question between equals in power while the strong do what they can and the weak suffer what they must.

When Thucydides adduced that the strong would do what they can, he assumed they would be motivated by greed leading them to exploit to the maximum extent possible weaker powers that lack the strength to resist effectively. By claiming that the weak would suffer what they must, he is deducing that exploitation would inevitably result in the suffering of people in weaker countries who have no power to end it while the strong countries ignore the safety, security and welfare of the exploited people in their pursuit of greed.

All the examples examined in detail in the chapters ahead attest to the exactitude of Thucydides' observation. His words serve as a paradigm for the relationship between strong and weak nations or groups.

Tragically, African nations were among those weak nations who suffered unconscionable atrocities at the hands of more powerful nations, and in particular, the United States since World War II.

CHAPTER 1

The Congo

Considered the worst humanitarian disaster since WW II, atrocities in the Congo can be attributed at least, partly, to the United States. The Congo was one of the keys to America's foreign policy's objective to replace the French as the dominant power in Central Africa. Central Africa is blessed with an abundance of resources, some of them vital for manufacturing electronic products.

In the process of pursuing this objective, the United States used Rwanda and Uganda as surrogate armies for the invasion of the Congo where many of the resources were located. These countries joined forces with a local insurgency in order to overthrow the government but in their effort to gain control of the Congo, at least six other countries such as Angola and the Sudan were drawn into the conflict resulting in what many historians refer to as the Third World War in Africa.

Tragically, the conflict in the Congo resulted in approximately six million civilian deaths, hundreds of thousands of rape victims, massive displacement of the population, a tremendous loss of resource wealth and zero development.

The crisis originated when nationalist riots threatened Belgium's control over the Democratic Republic of the Congo and it was granted independence on June 30, 1960. Patrice Lumumba was elected the first Prime Minister in the embryonic democracy but by declaring his neutrality during the Cold War and harboring dangerous beliefs such as socialism, his tenure became problematic and led to his assassination sixty-seven days later. His assassination remains somewhat of a mystery but it is known that Eisenhower ordered Allan Dulles, Director of the CIA, to eliminate Lumumba.

Mobutu, his replacement, a U.S. hand-picked dictator, was installed as president in 1965 and was heavily subsidized militarily by the U.S. in the amount of $1.5 billion from 1965 to 1991. Notwithstanding his corruption and brutality, American support was forthcoming by virtue of his anti-communism and his penchant for supporting the American agenda in Africa.

A central tenet in American objectives in Africa was to capitalize on its Congolese, Rwandan and Ugandan allies to secure control of Central Africa mainly for the rich repository of resources particularly in the Eastern Congo.

To strengthen their control over the resource-rich Eastern Congo, U.S. policy-makers decided to establish allies in Uganda and Rwanda who would inevitably invade the Congo as proxies of the United States.

President Museveni of Uganda was to become a strong ally of the United States by providing them with a strong proxy army to pursue both Ugandan and American interests.

In Museveni's pursuit of power, he stormed Kampala and overthrew President Milton Obote in 1986 with 3,000 Tutsi fighters who had become refugees from the Hutu government in Rwanda. These same exiles had wanted to return to Rwanda but were denied the right of return. In 1987, leading exiles decided to resort to force if necessary and formed the Rwanda Patriotic Front (RPF) with an armed wing known as the Rwanda Patriotic Army (RPA).

In 1990, the RPA launched an attempt to gain control of Rwanda by means of guerrilla attacks but with the intervention of the French, who also had ambitions in Rwanda, RPA soldiers were forced to retreat into Uganda.

New life was breathed into the RPA when Paul Kagame, an exiled Tutsi from Rwanda and a major in the Ugandan army, became the leader of the RPF. By 1991 he had organized the RPA into a disciplined guerrilla force of 5,000 men.

Kagame and the RPA resumed the civil war by conducting guerrilla raids into Rwanda eventually leading to a cease-fire due to pressure from the international community to end any future fighting between the RPA and the Hutu government in Rwanda. On August 24, 1993, the Arusha Accords were agreed to by the RPF and Rwandan government which called for a ceasefire and participation by the current five parties in the Rwanda government and the RPF.

Nevertheless, the RPF continued its efforts to defeat the Hutu government in Rwanda and ultimate victory can be partly attributed to the United States who was determined to establish allies in both Uganda and Rwanda. American leaders did not want a coalition government of Hutus and Tutsis in Rwanda as demanded in the Arusha Accords since they felt that the Hutus might not be amenable to the American agenda. To avert a coalition government, the U.S. supported Paul Kagame in his invasions of Rwanda. According to Global Research: "From 1989 onwards, America supported joint RPF-Ugandan attacks on Rwanda." (Michel Chossudovsky, *The US was behind the Rwandan Genocide: Installing a US Protectorate in Central Africa*, Global Research, April 7, 2010)

The U.S. armed Paul Kagame to enable him to organize a militia, the RPA, for the purpose of invading Rwanda and to gain control of the country. As well, Barrie Collins, Author on African affairs and contributor to "Rethinking Human Rights" stated that:

> The war waged by Uganda was facilitated by the United States in various ways... In addition to supporting the style of governance pursued by these leaders, the United States also supported them as proxies. (Barrie Collins, *In the waiting room of the Rwandan Genocide Tribunal*, May 26, 2006)

There were several methods used to support Museveni and Kagame financially enabling them to buy the weaponry needed for their invasion of Rwanda. One method was through the World Bank and the International Monetary Fund whose loans to these countries were diverted to the purchase of weapons. In 1986, the Uganda external debt totalled $1.3 billion dollars but climbed to $3.7 billion by 1997. Despite the requirement that each country fully reveal the allocation of the money in their budgets:

The donors had allowed defense spending to increase without impediment. The Ugandan external debt was being used to finance these military operations [in the Congo] on behalf of Washington.." (Michel Chossudovsky, The US was behind the Rwandan Genocide: Installing a US Protectorate in Central Africa, Global Research, April 7, 2010)

In addition, the United States provided $183 million in economic aid between 1989 and 1992 which was also diverted to military purchases to finance the invasion of Rwanda. (Barrie Collins, *In the waiting room of the Rwandan Genocide Tribunal*, May 26, 2006)

Kagame's insurgency eventually succeeded and his ascendancy to president coincided with the end of the genocide in 1994. The RPF formed its own government and was immediately recognized by the U.S. who established strong military ties with Rwanda in order to prepare for the invasion of Zaire (formerly the Congo).

One of the consequences of the genocide and civil war in Rwanda was the inundation of refugees into Zaire. During the genocide approximately one million Tutsis and moderate Hutus fled into Zaire to escape the machetes of the extreme Hutus responsible for the genocide. When Kagame and the Tutsis took over the Rwandan government, about one hundred thousand extreme Hutus fled to escape the fierce vengeance of the new government in Rwanda.

Once both Museveni and Kagame were in power, the United States was ready to direct its attention to a valuable prize, Zaire. (Mobutu changed the name from the Democratic Republic of the Congo to Zaire). Rwanda and Uganda were poor countries and could benefit from purloining the large repository of resources in Eastern Congo but they were also serving the interests of their ally, the U.S. In addition, Rwanda was motivated by a preoccupation with capturing the extreme Hutus who sought refuge in Zaire after Kagame took power in Rwanda. During a hearing before the House Subcommittee on International Operations and Human Rights on May 17, 2001, Wayne Madsen, journalist and author, reported that: "It is my observation that America's early support for Laurent Kabila [leader of the insurgency], which was aided by U.S. allies in Rwanda and Uganda, [was to open] up Congo's vast mineral riches to North American mining companies."

In addition, on July 10, 2003, Human Rights Watch reported that: "The U.S. government also has unique responsibilities for the crisis in the Congo. Two countries most valued in the conflict, Rwanda and Uganda, are two of Washington's closest allies on the continent."

Museveni and Kagame needed someone to be the next possible president to replace Mobutu in Zaire on whose behalf Rwanda and Uganda were ostensibly carrying out their intervention. They chose Laurent-Désiré Kabila, a former small-time guerrilla with a small fiefdom in the mountains in South Kivu who had become a smuggler in gold, ivory and leopard skins.

Internal opposition to Mobutu's rule provided the U.S., Rwanda and Uganda with a local fighting force to legitimatize the intervention. Two tribes who were a major factor in the resistance to Mobutu's rule were the Banyamulenge, Tutsi immigrants to the Congo before Congolese independence and the Banyarwanda who were also Tutsis who immigrated to the Congolese after independence.

The Banyamulenge were provoked into a rebellion in Zaire's eastern province of Kivu by the extremist Hutus who were responsible for the genocide in Rwanda and were now initiating a similar mass murder in their new home. As well, the deputy governor of Kivu ordered all Banyamulendge to leave Zaire within a week or face serious consequences.

Due to hatred of Mobutu's rule, the rebellion began to attract mass public support. These resistance fighters formed the alliance of Democratic Forces for the Liberation of Congo (AFDL) under the leadership of Kabila. Rwanda was a driving force in the organization of this new group and RPA soldiers joined the resistance.

In 1996, Kagame trained the AFDL in preparation for war against Mobutu and also prepared RPA troops in Rwanda for the intervention. U.S. provided military aid as revealed in an Amnesty International report:

> During 1996 and 1997 Uganda troops were reported to have assisted AFDL forces, particularly in northeastern Zaire, in response to the presence of Uganda armed opposition groups based in eastern Zaire. Uganda has close military links with Rwanda and the USA and has since 1990 been a conduit for military supplies to Rwanda and Burundi, which reportedly reached the AFDL. (*Democratic Republic of Congo: A long-standing crisis spinning out of control*, September 3, 1998)

One of the ways in which the United States contributed to a successful intervention in Zaire was by providing training for the invading troops. Green Berets from the 3rd Special Forces Group based at Fort Bragg, N.C., actively trained RPA forces, a continuation of the training they had received prior to 1994. Keith Snow wrote for Human Rights Watch that the Washington Post (July 12, 1998) revealed that:

> Far from being an innocent bystander...the United States not only gave Kagame $75 million in military assistance, but also sent Green Berets to train Kagame's forces (as well as their Uganda rebel allies) in low intensity conflict (LIC) tactics. (*The Rwanda Genocide Fabrications*, April 6, 2009)

As well, Ellen Ray wrote that:

> Is it a coincidence that Rwanda strongman Paul Kagame was trained in the United States? That the Rwandan army received, and continues to receive, training in the U.S.? That the Pentagon has Special Forces military training missions in Rwanda and Uganda for more than five years? (*U.S. Military and Corporate Recolonization of the Congo*, Covert Action Quarterly, Spring/Summer 2000)

Once the invasion had commenced, to ensure success of the operation, the U.S. maintained regular contact with Kabila through the U.S. embassy in Kigali (capital of Rwanda).

Resistance by Mobutu and his army was very ineffectual due to the tensions of different ethnic groups in Zaire, strong resistance to his corrupt leadership, an army that was forced to prey upon the population for survival and the ease with which rebel groups could find refuge in Zaire.

Banishing the Banyamulenge from Zaire was the trigger for Kagame who used their uprising as a pretext for the invasion in the province of South Kivu where he captured the provincial capital of Bukavu.

Then the AFDL marched northward until they captured Goma, the provincial capital of North Kivu.

Refugee camps dotted the territory surrounding Goma providing a sanctuary for 60,000 of the extreme Hutus who upon the advent of the AFDL hastily fled back into Rwanda although tens of thousands of refugees were massacred by the AFDL before they could escape.

AFDL forces continued their advance toward their ultimate objective, Kinshasa, the capital of Zaire, virtually unopposed due to the poorly trained, unpaid and disloyal forces of Mobutu. During the march, one town after another was defeated by the rebels and many local militias joined forces with the AFDL.

Angola joined forces with the AFDL out of resentment of Mobutu's support for the Angolan rebel leader Jonas Savimbi and his Unita Movement. Thet also wanted to eliminate Unita fighters who were stationed in Zaire as a base for raids into Angola.

A growing number of militias were joining the fray, all of whom needed food, shelter and women. Local Hutus and Tutsis, Rwanda, Ugandan and Angolan forces, some of whom were fighting with the AFDL and Mobutu's ragtag group of soldiers, were scattered all over Zaire, rendering every village in the country unsafe. Women and girls, in particular, paid a very high price and young boys were recruited as porters and soldiers.

During the month of April 1997, the AFDL continued to capture town after town on its march towards Kinshasa. On May 16, 1997, Kabila gained control of the Lubumbashi airport and Mobutu fled the country. Kabila declared himself president on September 7, 1997 renaming the country the Democratic Republic of the Congo (DRC).

Once in office, Kabila proudly announced that he was the second coming of Lumumba and would dedicate himself to the task of freeing the people of the Congo. In reality, he proved to be a totally incompetent leader who mistakenly refused to work with any of the opposition groups and who also banned political parties.

Rather than freeing the people of the Congo, he created a security apparatus and military court to try civilians who defied his restrictions on political activities.

In May 1998, he nationalized a major Congolese railway thereby frightening investors and furthering suspicions that his policies would reflect his Marxist beliefs. He was also perceived as barely differing from his predecessor as he was characterized as authoritarian, corrupt and indifferent to human rights.

Furthermore, there was considerable public resentment concerning the number of Rwandans in Kabila's inner circle.

Finally, Kabila ordered Rwandan and Ugandan military forces to leave the country provoking Museveni and Kagame to plot another regime change in Kinshasa. On August 2, 1998, the Banyamulenge with the support of Rwandan and Ugandan forces rose up in mutiny against Kabila. The rebels formed a group called the Rally for Congolese Democracy (RCD) who rapidly gained control of the resource-rich eastern provinces.

After early successes in Kivu, including the towns of Goma, Bukavu and Uvira, Rwandan commanders organized a massive airlift of troops from Goma to Kitona, just west of Kinshasa.

A number of Kabila's soldiers abandoned him and joined the rebellion as they marched towards Kinshasa. RCD forces gained control of the hydroelectric station that supplied power to Kinshasa and the port of Matadi through which most of Kinshasa's food passed. By late August, the rebel forces began to threaten the capital.

Fortunately for Kabila, his diplomatic efforts with the South African Development Community (SADC) paid dividends when the governments of Namibia, Zimbabwe and Angola rushed to his rescue. Angola's primary objective was to prevent an opportunity for the Unita forces to re-establish rear bases in the Congo for attacks on Angola. As well, both Eduardo dos Santos of Angola and Robert Mugabe of Zimbabwe aspired to be regional power brokers. All these countries hoped to enrich themselves with the enormous bounty of resources in the Congo.

Repercussion of Rwanda's and Uganda's second invasion was a virtual world war within the Congo where all the countries involved grabbed whatever spoils were available. Angola took control of oil production and distribution while Zimbabwe established joint ventures in diamonds, gold and timber.

Although Rwanda and Uganda failed to dislodge Kabila from power in Kinshasa, they turned eastern Congo into their own domain where they plundered for gold, diamonds, timber, coltan and coffee.

On the other hand, Burundi's Tutsi government decided to join Rwanda and Uganda to protect its borders against Hutu rebel groups in the Congo.

In the following weeks, the governments of Chad, Libya and Sudan also decided to support Kabila.

The result of the World War in Africa was that between 1998 and 2002, four million people died. Women were raped, villages destroyed, young girls kidnapped to be concubines and young boys were recruited to serve as soldiers and porters.

Much of the responsibility for the war can be attributed to the corporations who were illegally purchasing resources from the various national armies who were able to finance their continued operation of the war with the money earned from these sales. The invading countries had no rights to these resources which legally belonged to the people of the Congo. Not only did they lose their resources but suffered unconscionable human rights abuses by these militias. According to Dena Montague in the John Hopkins School of Advanced International Studies (SAIS) Review:

> Rebel movements have been able to successfully sustain their war efforts by plundering and looting the economic wealthy of the country's mineral-rich eastern region. The Uganda People's defense Forces (UPDF) and the Rwandan Patriotic Army (RPA), as well as the Congolese rebels they each support-the Rally for Congolese Democracy (RCD) and Congolese Liberation Front (CLF)-have ruthlessly exploited the mineral wealth from territories under their respective control. (SAIS Review, *Stolen Goods: Coltan and Conflict in the Democratic Republic of the Congo*, Winter-Spring, 2002)

For example, in the late 1990's, demand for coltan escalated due to the development of a whole range of new electronic products such as cell phones and PCs, raising its value. Eighty percent of all coltan is located in the Congo. United States corporations such as Cabot Corporation, OM group, Bechtel, AVX, American Mineral Fields, Eagle Wings Resources International and Trinitech International have been, in the words of the UN, "the engine of conflict in the DRC". These corporations import coltan from Rwanda by means of transactions that lack a certification process thus rendering it impossible to trace the origin of the coltan. The SAIS Review claims that:

> The Rwandan and Ugandan companies have monopolies mined in their respective territories. Middlemen are hired from relationships with western clients, and they facilitate transactions between these companies and foreign corporations without questioning the legitimacy of the DRC-based transactions. Coltan sales have earned Uganda and Rwanda multi-million dollar revenues, which each has used to sustain their respective war efforts in eastern DRC. (ibid)

Mining executives were directly involved in the purchasing of coltan by flying into the DRC in their private jets to negotiate contracts with officials acting on behalf of Rwanda or Uganda. For example, Jean Ramon Boulle, co-founder of American Mineral Fields arrived in the DRC in April 1997 to negotiate a one billion dollar deal with rebels and during his visit allowed the rebels to use his private Lear jet. Another example involves Bechtel which conducted satellite studies for the AFDL using their personal satellite for the purpose of defining the mineral potential of the Congo. Bechtel satellite surveillance was also useful to Kabila in developing military strategy.

Until the AFDL invasion of Zaire in 1996, exports of coltan from Rwanda to the United States dropped from $3 million in 1993 to $598,000 in 1995 but more than doubled from 1997 to 2000. Ugandan exports reached a high of $645,000 by 1999. (ibid)

The 1998 invasion by Rwanda and Uganda was an attempt to overthrow Kabila. Kabila, as mentioned earlier was saved by a number of states but the fighting continued nevertheless. In September of 1998, Zimbabwean forces were airlifted into Kinshasa and thwarted the rebel advance. Angolan forces attacked northward from its borders thus forcing the rebel forces to retreat.

To exacerbate an already terror-ridden conflict amongst all the different forces fighting each other, infighting between Rwanda and Uganda forces ignited over coltan-rich areas in the Eastern Congo. Tensions reached a breaking point in early August when the two armies clashed in Kisangani.

On January 19, 1999, Rwanda, Uganda, Angola, Namibia and Zimbabwe met in Windhoek, Namibia, and agreed to a ceasefire but the RCD refused to sign any agreement unless Kabila was directly involved in the talks. They argued that the conflict was primarily internal and no agreement would be viable without the participation of the Congolese leader.

On April 9, 1999, the United Nations responded to the multi-national conflict in the Congo with Resolution 1234 deploring "the presence of foreign states in the [DRC]".

Following the failed attempt to consummate a ceasefire agreement, the Organization of African Unity and Southern African Development Community held numerous meetings in order to pressure the various parties to reach an accord. Uganda and Rwanda sheathed their swords under further pressure from the United States who was financing both armies.

New terms of a ceasefire were drawn up when foreign and defense ministers met in Lusaka in July 1999. All parties to the conflict, including the DRC, Namibia, Angola, Zimbabwe, Burundi, Rwanda and Uganda attended. The RCD and the Movement for the Liberation of the Congo (MLC), backed by Uganda, only endorsed the agreement. Finally, on August 1, 1999, the MLC signed the agreement and the RCD signed it on August 31.

Its terms included immediate cessation of hostilities, disarming of identified militias, to monitor the withdrawal of foreign troops and to respect the deployment of a Chapter VII UN force.

Ongoing clashes between Rwanda and Uganda prompted the United Nations to pass Resolution 1304 in 2000 which noted "with concern reports of the illegal exploitation of the country's assets and the potential consequences of these actions on security conditions and the continuation of hostilities."

On February 24, 2000, United Nations Resolution 1291 authorized a Chapter VII deployment of a maximum of 5547 troops in the Congo including 500 military observers. Under the authority of this Resolution, the Security Council mandated the mission to take the necessary action to ensure the protection of civilians under the threat of imminent violence.

By December of 2000, only 224 military personnel were deployed due to the lack of security in the DRC and the reluctance of the Congolese government to accept UN troops. The peacekeeping group, known as the United Nations Organization and Destabilization Mission in the Democratic Republic of Congo (MONUC) eventually rose to 17,000 troops.

Notwithstanding the ceasefire agreement, Uganda and Rwanda persisted in their scramble for resources in the eastern Congo when on three occasions they fought for control of Kisangani. Rebel groups also continued to attack government forces.

Kabila's frustration was escalating in trying to rule a country beset on all sides by Ugandan, Rwandan and rebel forces which were either battling themselves or his government. In an effort to end the fighting, Kabila called on the Security Council to strongly condemn the violations of the ceasefire and to demand the immediate withdrawal of Ugandan and Rwandan forces.

Originally, Kabila had regarded the Ugandan and Rwandan forces as allies working with him to oust Mobutu but it had now become clear to him that they were pursuing their own self-interest in staking out territory from which they could steal resources.

To add to the chaos, Kabila was assassinated by a young member of his body guard on January 16 2001. There was no obvious replacement upon whom Kabila's top staff could agree, so they settled on his 30-year old son, Joseph, who had been serving in the army as the chief-of-staff. Joseph had little experience in politics and no power base. Surprisingly, he was very decisive, lifting the ban on political parties and opening a dialogue with his rivals.

In 2002, three peace agreements were negotiated and signed by the parties to the agreement which created conditions in which the Congo might potentially achieve stability, peace and growth.

On July 30, 2002, Rwanda and the DRC signed an agreement known as the Pretoria Accord which required Rwanda to withdraw approximately 20,000 troops from the Congo and to round up and dismantle the Hutu militia who had sought refuge in the Congo after perpetrating the genocide in Rwanda.

Then on September 6, 2002, Uganda and the DRC reached an accord known as the Luanda Agreement requiring Uganda to withdraw its troops from the Congo and formalizing peace between the two countries.

After two weeks of negotiations in South Africa, rebel forces in the DRC signed the Global All-Inclusive Agreement on December 17, 2002 after four years of a civil war fraught with terror for the civilian population. During the war, there were seven foreign armies in the DRC numbering at least 50,000, between two and three million people died, disease and rape were rampant, and hundreds of thousands of people were displaced.

Congolese parties who signed the agreement included the national government, the MLC, RCD, domestic political opposition, representatives of civil society and the Mai-Mai. The Mai-Mai were a community-based group formed to defend their territory, mainly in the Kivus, against other armed groups but who ultimately exploited the war for their own purposes, namely to sell resources.

The accord specified that Kabila and four vice-presidents would lead a transitional government for 18 months to be followed by a referendum and then democratic elections. Parliamentary seats and cabinet positions would be shared among opposition parties and rebel forces to ensure that all parties seeking power would have a stake in the government. Zimbabwe and Angola respected the peace initiative and withdrew their troops as well.

Testing the effectiveness of the accord would be measured by the willingness of the various militia forces to integrate into government forces. Success of the agreement would ensure stability in the Congo ending the horrific human rights abuses and allowing the government to engage in the implementation of progressive policies.

Regrettably for the Congolese people, Kabila did not respect the spirit or terms of the agreement thereby leading the Congo into further conflict. Despite the ostensible power-sharing with all opposition groups, Kabila controlled the central state apparatus and most of the country's revenues. As well, various militias refuse to lay down their arms so that they could retain control over valuable territory.

Despite agreement in the peace accord that signatories would be entitled to positions in important institutions such as the central bank, Supreme Court, the two largest state-owned mining companies and the intelligence service, Kabila refused to comply.

Not surprisingly, the RCD withdrew from the transitional process in August 2004 and the MLC threatened to withdraw in January 2005 but Kabila successfully called their bluff. Without the support of their former patrons, they lost their military prowess and suffered a loss of their territory as Mai-Mai militias supported by Kinshasa usurped much of their territory in the East. It was now forced to enter the political process in order to regain any power in the Congo. Transition to a political party as an addition to its military wing was very problematic since many of the leaders of the RCD distanced themselves from the Hutu and Tutsi leadership.

Attempts to reintegrate the Eastern Congo met with resistance from Rwanda and its rebel forces who were not prepared to cede all the resource-rich territories to Kinshasa. Some RCD leaders led by Brigadier General Laurent Nkunda were hardliners who refused any integration with the DRC. Nkunda was a former warlord operating in North Kivu who was sympathetic to the Congolese Tutsis and the Tutsi-dominated government in Rwanda. He was an intelligence officer in the Rwandan army and former commander of several brigades in the Congolese army. Another warlord and rebel leader, Jules Mutebutsi, was a former officer in the RCD and a Tutsi from South Kivu.

Hope for peace and stability when the 2006 elections were underway was threatened by these dissatisfied elements of the RCD, especially in North Kivu, where they have repeatedly attacked other militias causing the displacement of 50,000 to 70,000 civilians.

Several factors have contributed to the continued operations of militias in the eastern Congo. Lack of control over the Congolese army has rendered it possible for 14,000 to 18,000 militiamen to terrorize the population in the east. As well, weakness in the UN forces has also created opportunities for militias in the east. Chapter VII peacekeepers now numbered 17,000 but were unable to engage in counterinsurgency operations due to the risk of suffering extensive casualties and to their lack of numbers. For example, in June 2004, Nkunda's and Mutebutsi's forces attacked and captured the eastern town of Bukavu killing numerous civilians and forced the MONUC forces to flee the town.

Another factor was the availability of arms and ammunition supplied by a number of countries including the United States. A report from the International Action Network on Small Arms stated that: "Bullets manufactured in Greece, China, Russia and the USA have been found in the Ituri District of eastern Democratic Republic of Congo (DRC), which is under a UN embargo." (International Action Network, *Bullets from Greece...and United States Found in Rebel Hands in DRC*, October 16, 2006)

One of the major horrific consequences of these ubiquitous militias was rape, inflicted on women and men, indiscriminate of age. In South Kivu alone approximately 42,000 women were treated at health clinics for serious sexual assaults in 2005. According to the Guardian: "Doctors and women's groups working with the victims say the attacks are notable not only for their scale but also their brutality." (Chris McGreal, *Hundreds of Thousands Raped in the Congo*, Guardian, November 13, 2006)

Expectations for the upcoming referendum in 2005 and election in 2006 was problematic for the people of the Congo given the past history of violence, instability and inexorable disagreement among conflicting parties. Their worst fears were realized as the outcome of the election, if anything, deepened the divisions among the opposing political and military groups. Disaster reigned supreme yet one more time for the constantly terrorized and deprived population.

During the entire electoral process, conflict raged in parts of the Congo. The RCD militia mutinied in Rutshuru in North Kivu and the Mai-Mai clashed with the newly integrated army (FARDC) in the Kivus and Katanga in 2005 and 2006.

Despite the pessimism, 25.6 million voters registered for the referendum on a new constitution in 2005 and 70% actually voted. The result was an 84% vote to approve the new constitution.

In the first set of elections since 1960, Kabila took 45% of the votes and his main opponent, Jean-Pierre Bemba took 20% but since neither presidential candidate won more than 50% of the votes, a runoff election was necessary. In the runoff election, Kabila won 58% of the vote thus winning the presidency.

Bemba was one of four vice-presidents in the transitional government following his leadership of the MLC rebel group, which out of necessity, created a political wing.

The election results were condemned as rigged by Bemba and he refused to accept the results. In Kinshasa, where Bemba won a majority of the votes, there was widespread belief that the election results did not reflect the voter's intentions. UN peacekeepers requested that Bemba's forces return to their barracks but they refused.

Rather than uniting the country, the election results stirred up deep-seated animosity and led to more violence.

Kabila won over 80% of the vote in the East while Bemba won by a similar margin in the western provinces. One exacerbated division was based on the enmity of the Swahili-speaking east which backed Kabila, while the west, especially Kinshasa, rejected him on ethnic grounds and perceived him as a foreign puppet. Western provinces resented Kabila for failing to address important social problems such as poverty, education and health care. Unemployment was close to 80% and many families ate only one meal a day.

Another source of hostility in the west was the political marginalization of the opposition which was largely based in the west and Bemba, who won 42% of the popular vote, was too weak in the national assembly to challenge the ruling alliance. The danger of alienating the opposition in a country torn by strife is that opposition supporters will take to the streets. In January, 2007, when one losing opposition candidate's supporters took to the streets and clashed with the police, the governor was forced into calling in the army leading to the death of more than one hundred civilians.

Kinshasa was a hotbed of latent enmity towards Kabila and his ruling alliance. In March, 2007, Bemba's militia of four to five hundred soldiers forced a confrontation with the army, plunging the capital into bloody violence. Human rights groups estimated the death toll at around 500 civilians. The result was a further clamp down on dissidents and opposition groups who were subject to arrest on dubious charges such as treason and detained. Several television stations belonging to the opposition were shut down.

Elites and foreign mining companies now had a vested interest in undermining stability and lack of a strong central government in order to continue benefitting from profits from procurement contracts and mining deals. There was ongoing neglect of social services including health care, education, alleviation of poverty and reduction of unemployment.

Between the elections in 2006 and 2011 was a period of constant conflicts and battles causing numerous deaths, subjecting the local population to rape and kidnapping or forcing a myriad of civilians to seek refuge. At the same time, the weakness and lack of motivation of Kabila and his central government deprived the Congolese people of any improvements in their standard of living and denied them security and stability relegating them to the life of suffering, fear and misery that has characterized their life since 1960.

It is important to recall that this cycle of violence and the concomitant suffering was triggered by the United States and Belgium when they assassinated Lumumba and supported ruthless dictators since the destruction of the Congo's first democratic government. Speculation about the fate of the DRC had Lumumba lived is not known or even predictable but the action of the U.S. and other countries clearly opened the trap door to hell and guaranteed many horrible years of suffering.

As well as assassinating the first democratically leader in the Congo, the United States and other countries were responsible for supporting brutal and corrupt dictators with arms and other forms of aid. These dictators include Mobutu, Museveni and Kagame who were supported by the U.S. as client states so that they could invade the DRC to purloin its vast resources for themselves and their superpower sponsor.

Multinational corporations are equally guilty for purchasing the resources from agents or directly from Rwanda, the revenues from which financed the ongoing occupation of the eastern Congo by several predatory states and militias.

To describe in detail the events between the two elections is an unnecessary exercise but a brief description of the various militias involved in the conflicts followed by a summary of events is described below provide you with an awareness of life in the Congo during this period.

Militias and Armies

1. FARDC or DRC forces refer to the Congolese government army;
2. FDLR stands for the Democratic Forces for the Liberation of Rwanda and is a HUTU group;
3. CNDP is the Tutsi under the command of Nkunda and secretly funded by Rwanda;
4. MONUC is the United Nations Chapter VII peacekeeping force;
5. RCD is a Tutsi rebel group;

6. Mai-Mai is a rebel group whose purpose was to protect its territory and it often sided with the government;

7. CNDP splinter group which broke away from Nkunda and was led by Mukbusi.

The following events are a sample of the conflicts and battles between the two elections which occurred mostly in the Kivus or surrounding towns and cities.

<u>Battles and Conflicts 2006 to 2011</u>

- 2006 January - CNDP clash with DRC forces around the town of Sake
- 2006 November 25 - CNDP takes sake in battle against DRC forces and MONUC
- 2006 December 7 - RCD attack DRC forces in North Kivu- DRC forces and MONUC regain positions - 12,000 civilians flee
- 2007 September – CNDP fights DRC forces in Masisi north of Goma
- 2007 – September 5- Nkunda calls for peace
- 2007 – Nkunda raids 10 secondary schools and four primary schools – took children by force – girls taken as sex slaves – boys used as soldiers
- 2007 – October 7 – DRC forces allied with Mai-Mai advance on Nkunda's stronghold of Kichanga – thousands of civilians flee
- 2007 – number of people displaced since the beginning of the year was 370,000
- 2007 – December – DRC forces capture the town of Mushake

- 2007 – December 14 – Nkunda calls for peace talks
- 2008 – January 23 – peace deal is signed among DRC and militias
- 2008 – DRC forces and MONUC decide to remove FDLR forces from Kivu
- 2008 – CNDP forces declare war on FDLR
- 2008 – October 26 – CNDP captures a major military camp belonging to DRC forces for use as a base
- 2008 - MONUC attack helicopters were used in an effort to halt rebel advance who are very near Goma
- 2008 – October 28 – combined forces of DRC and MONUC battle against rebels between the Kimumba refugee camp and Rutshuru – Rebels capture the town – civilians riot against DRC forces in frustration for the lack of progress
- 2008 – October 29 – Rebel forces declare ceasefire as they approach Goma
- 2008 – October 30 – looting and violence by Congolese soldiers continues into Goma
- 2008 – October 30 – Nkunda calls for a ceasefire
- 2008 – November 6 – Nkunda and CNDP break ceasefire and capture Nyanzak army base
- 2008 – November – CNDP and DRC forces clash around Goma
- 2009 – January 9 – Rwanda army in joint operation with DRC forces capture Nkunda who is held in Rwanda. He is replaced by Bosco Ntaganda
- 2009 – March 23 – Rwanda and DRC forces joint operation against Hutu militia responsible for Rwandan genocide comes to an end – CNDP agrees to become a political party – Kivu conflict ended

- 2009 – May 9/10 – FDLR attack villages in Ekingi and Busurungi in Congo's eastern South Kivu province – DRC forces and MONUC plan operations in South Kivu to eliminate the FDLR
- 2010 – August 24 – FDLR and Mai-Mai rape and assault at least 154 civilians in town of Luvungi

Unconscionable human right's violations had been a curse for the people of the Congo since the death of Lumumba but the scale and depth of suffering was at its nadir since 1997.

When seven countries and numerous militias were fighting each other or the government, tens of thousands of soldiers, all of whom were either not paid or paid very little, were on the move throughout the Congo. When they would enter a town or village, it was almost inevitable that they would steal food, rape women and take women or girls and boys with them to be used as soldiers, porters or concubines.

Multifarious forces prowling about the country also triggered the inundation of refugees seeking safety in the jungle where there was no food or clean water. In the jungle, hundreds of thousands of refugees either died or became severely ill.

Compounding the problem was the paucity of food and medical assistance from international agencies due to lack of money or safety when flying aid to hostile territories. Even very treatable diseases or injuries could not be attended to due to this shortage.

For example, Father Jean Pierre, an Italian Priest, devoted several years of his life trying to assist the people and refugees in the town of Shabunda which is located west of Goma in the jungle. All the women in the town had been raped, some as many as seven times suffering terrible injuries as a result. Most of the children were malnourished, many of whom were not expected to live. While he was there, only one plane carrying food flew into Shabunda which was near some of the heaviest fighting.

Tens of thousands of women and girls have been raped by members of the Congolese army, rebel militias or individual citizens. (Human Rights Watch, *Soldiers Who Rape, Commanders Who Condone*, July 16 2009) According to the United Nations Population Fund (UNFPA), a UN agency dedicated to the prevention of rape: "15,996 new cases of sexual violence were registered in 2008 throughout the country. In the eastern provinces of North Kivu alone, there were 4,820 new cases." (UNFPA, *Figures on sexual violence reported in the DRC in 2008*, 2008)

Amnesty International reports that in 2004, 40,000 cases of rape had been reported over the previous six years in South Kivu. The number of rape victims is difficult to estimate due to lack of access to many of the conflict areas but one estimate of surviving rape victims throughout the Congo is as many as 400,000. (Kira Cochrane, *The Victims Witness*, The Guardian, 2009)

Sexual assault has lasting effects such as long-term psychological, health and social ramifications for the victims in the Kivus. HIV, long-term health complications and unwanted pregnancies are some of the risks of rape as well as the impact on young girls who face the prospect of rejection as a wife or the need to drop out of school.

Rape was not only sexual in nature but a tool of war used against women, families or entire communities. Sometimes rape was used as a means to exert control over civilian populations (Amnesty International, *Democratic Republic of Congo: Making a Killing*, October 22, 2002) or a method of punishing perceived or real alliances with rebel army factions (Amnesty International, 2009).

Overall, the number of rapes is mind-numbing. According to the American Journal of Public Health:

Approximately 1.69 to 1.80 million women reported having been raped in their lifetime (with 407,397-433,785 women reporting having been raped in the preceding 12 months), and approximately 3.07 to 3.37 million women reported experiencing intimate partner sexual violence. (Amber Peterman, PhD, Tia Palermo, PhD and Caryn BredenKamp, PhD. *Estimates and Determinants of Sexual Violence Against Women in the Democratic Republic of Congo*, June 2011, Vol. 101, No. 6)

The Journal also reports that:

Violence against women, often used as a systematic tactic of war to destabilize populations and destroy community and family bonds, has become more common and increasingly brutal in recent years in the Democratic Republic of Congo (DRC). Reports from the DRC indicate that sexual violence is widespread and includes gang rape, forced participation of family members in rape, and mutilation of women's genitalia with knives and guns, among other atrocities. (ibid)

Deaths during the period 1998 to 2002 ranks the war in the Congo as the worst human rights disaster since World War II. Overwhelmingly, these deaths were not a direct result of violence but were due to forced living in the jungle where food and clean water was in very short supply and disease was rampant. As expected, the vulnerability of children is reflected in the death statistics. According to the International Rescue Committee (IRC): "Based on the results of the five IRC studies, we now estimate that 5.4 million excess deaths have occurred between August 1998 and April 2007." (International Rescue Committee, *Mortality in the Democratic Republic of the Congo: An Ongoing Crisis*, 2007)

Elaborating on the causes of death, the IRC explains that:

> The majority of deaths across DR Congo have been due to infectious diseases, malnutrition and neonatal and pregnancy-related conditions. Increased rates of diseases are likely related to social and economic disturbances caused by conflict, including disruption of health services, poor food security, deterioration of infrastructure and population displacement. Children, who are particularly susceptible to these easily preventable and treatable conditions, accounted for 47 percent of deaths, even though they contributed only 19 percent of the total population. (ibid)

When militias or even DRC forces were raping and pillaging their way through the Congo, population centres become quickly deserted when they are nearby in order to avoid the violence and rape that is horrifyingly imminent. According to Refugees International, there were 2.4 million internally displaced persons on the Congo as of November 12, 2012 and 460,000 have become refugees in neighbouring countries. (Refugees International, *DR Congo*, 2012) In addition to leaving their homes and worldly possessions behind, care is problematic in refugee camps because: "Access for humanitarian organizations to assist displaced populations remains extremely challenging due to ongoing insecurity and poor roads." (ibid)

Disease is the curse which refugees are faced with as well as insufficient food and few if any amenities. UNHCR states that:

> After surviving the trauma of forced displacement and insecurity, thousands of Congolese refugees are facing a new and potentially fatal danger in Uganda – malaria…But the resources to deal with this threat are limited. There is only one health centre to service a population of 30,000 refugees and 35,000 Ugandans living in and around the settlement. (UNHCR, *Rising malaria health threat for Congolese refugees in Uganda*, December 3, 2012)

Many other diseases and health problems have afflicted refugees who are enduring the hardships of war and refugee camps. The World Health Organization (WHO) has reported that:

> The humanitarian crisis in the Democratic Republic of Congo (DRC) has continued for more than 10 years. The population of the DRC lives in an environment of insecurity and poverty (70% of the population lives below the poverty line).
>
> Key health indicators such as mortality (540/100 000 live births) in the DRC are alarming. There is low access to basic health services and a continuation of major outbreaks of cholera, malaria and measles. According to the nutrition cluster 2,439,469 children suffer from malnutrition in the country. (World Health Organization, *Response to the crisis in the Democratic Republic of the Congo*, November, 2012)

As the 2011 elections were approaching, divisiveness prevailed throughout the country casting a dark shadow over the prospect of electing a government which might benefit all the people of the Congo. There was a strong possibility that if Kabila wins the election there will be massive protests throughout the country.

Opposition uprisings are very likely in Kinshasa, Lubumbashio, Bukavu, Mbuji-Mayi and Kananga leading to a harsh crackdown by security forces. As well as population protests, there are still armed militia groups in the east.

Among the reasons for strong opposition to Kabila's re-election is a track record in which he has failed to live up to his promises such as building infrastructure, providing access to clean water and electricity, improvements in health and education. As well, his record on civil and legal rights is very poor including the murder of journalists and NGO workers. He has also continued to allow predatory foreign corporations to steal Congolese resources.

Voters were so convinced that the election results were fixed that they challenged the entire electoral process by violent means. For example, gunmen opened fire on a truck carrying voting materials in Lubumbashi and later attacked voting centres. There were intimidations of voters, burning down of polling stations and Human Rights Watch claims that nine were killed in Kinshasa and 76 injured.

An insufficient level of preparation and suspicions of fraud delegitimized the election results announced in December 2011 with Kabila winning 49% of the vote and his challenger, Etienne Tshisekedi, winning 32%.

Confirming the suspicions of those who questioned the results of the elections, The American based Carter Center found that:

> The provisional presidential election results announced by the independent National Election Commission (CENI) on Dec. 9 in the Democratic Republic of the Congo lack credibility. Carter Centre observers reported that the quality and integrity of the tabulation process has varied across the country, ranging from the proper application of procedures to serious irregularities, including the loss of nearly 2,000 polling station results in Kinshasa... These and other observations point to mismanagement of the results process and compromise the integrity of the presidential election. (The Carter Center, *DRC Presidential Election Results Lack Credibility*, December 10, 2011)

The Carter Centre was founded by Jimmy and Rosalynn Carter and operates in conjunction with Emory University guided by a fundamental commitment to human rights.

After the election results were announced on December 9, 2001, Tshisekedi condemned the results as corrupt and replete with irregularities and immediately declared himself president. Violence broke out in Kinshasa following the election resulting in the police firing teargas to break up angry demonstrations.

Expectedly, the U.S. did not take a firm stand against Kabila since he was still serving American interests. Hillary Clinton, Secretary of State, issued a very mixed message that ultimately supported Kabila. She said that:

> We believe that the management and technical execution of these elections are seriously flawed, lacked transparency and did not measure up to the democratic

> gains we have seen in recent African elections. *However, it is still not clear whether the irregularities were sufficient to change the outcome of the election.* (Hillary Clinton, *Hillary Clinton on DRC Elections*, December 20, 2011

She criticized the DRC for election irregularities but then without knowledge of the impact of the irregularities other than the Carter report which called into question the integrity of the election, she gave Congo a pass because the outcome was probably not affected.

Without a strong, legitimate central government and a powerful army, all the ills plaguing the DRC were certain to continue.

Despite the March 23, 2009 peace agreement between the CNDP and the DRC government, calling for the CNDP to become a political party and to integrate its troops into the DRC forces, a new rebel group emerged from this agreement known as M23. It was formed on April 4, 2012 when 300 members of the former CNDP broke away from the DRC out of frustration that the government and army did not implement the terms of the agreement. The government was about to deploy many of these militiamen away from North Kivu which prompted their defection.

On November 20, M23 rebels managed to gain control of Goma, the provincial capital of North Kivu, forcing 140,000 people to flee their homes. There was little resistance and the United Nation's forces, MONUSCO, with 19,000 troops did not intervene. M23 forces, led by Gen. Bosco Ntanganda, former chief of staff of the CNDP and former member of the Rwanda Patriotic Army, expanded their control in the eastern Congo by capturing Rutshuru, just Northeast of Goma.

On July, 6, M23 captured the town Bunagana which was located less than a kilometer away from the Ugandan border. M23 was now closing in on Goma, the important capital of North Kivu.

In November, a heavy battle erupted in Goma as DRC forces used tanks and helicopters which didn't impede rebel forces on their march toward the city while MONUSCO forces used helicopter gunships.

On November 19, 2012, M23 forces launched their attack against Goma with mortar shells and machine gun fire while DRC forces were still there. On November 20, rebel forces advanced on foot towards the centre of the city eventually capturing most of the city. With DRC forces on the run and UN peacekeepers standing down, the city fell to M23 forces. At this point, the only tactic remaining to president Kabila was to urge the citizens of Goma to resist the rebel forces.

When 3,000 members of the DRC forces and police forces defected to M23 forces, it was a foreboding to Kabila of what lay ahead. M23 forces then captured the town of Sake and commenced marching toward Bukavu announcing their next target as Kisangani.

Kabila refused to wave the white flag and launched a counterattack on the city of Sake resulting in fierce fighting in the city. DRC forces were easily warded off and fled the city in disarray. Government forces demonstrated once again that they were not above looting, raping and threatening civilians.

An attempt at a peace agreement using the Chief of Uganda's defence forces as a mediator failed miserably as M23 forces refused to yield any ground. Subsequently, DRC forces treated the actions of M23 as a declaration of war and prepared to resume combat.

M23 forces finally agreed to withdraw from captured territory with a promise to eventually pull out of Goma. Under DRC forces control, the rebels abandoned Goma.

On November 18, DRC forces were compelled to withdraw.

To understand the success of M23 it is essential to identify which states are supporting them. According to Human Rights Watch: "the Rwandan army has deployed its troops to eastern Congo to directly support the M23 rebels in military operations." (Human Rights Watch, DR Congo: *M23 Rebels Committing War Crimes*, September 11, 2012)

A letter addressed to the President of the Security Council reports that Rwanda "is providing direct military support to the M23 rebels facilitating recruitment." Rwanda was also supplying arms, intelligence and ammunition to the rebels. (Chair: Group of Experts, *Letter to the President of the Security Council*, November 12, 2012)

As well, the letter states that the Government of Uganda was supporting M23 forces with direct troop replacements in the Congo, weapons deliveries and technical assistance.

M23 also expanded its forces by recruiting child soldiers as confirmed in the letter to the President of the Security Council who noted that: "The use and recruitment of child soldiers has increased by armed groups, notably by M23." (ibid)

United States support for both Uganda and Rwanda enabled them to support the M23 rebels. Although criticism for supporting armies who rape and use child soldiers compelled the United States to withhold $200,000 from the Rwanda government, the amount withheld pales in comparison to the $240 million offered as support to that very same government.

In addition to indirectly funding the armies engaged in such vile practices, American strategy was to hide the real facts of events in the Congo from the public. Susan Rice, American Ambassador to the United Nations, blocked the release of two reports that reveals, in all its depraved details, the crimes against humanity perpetrated by American friends including the forced displacement of another 650,000 people.

Clearly, an examination of all the causes of the crimes against humanity that have been occurring in the Congo since 1960 would be a challenging undertaking. One cause that does stand out is the role of the United States. By removing Lumumba from office and supporting the dictators who followed paved the way for the exploitation of resources that was unbelievably devastating to the Congo. Venal, corrupt and greedy dictators are much preferable to democracies when exploiting a country where millions are killed and millions more are displaced. It is much easier to bully or bribe a dictator than to convince a legislative assembly and executive body to commit crimes against their own people and serve the interests of the master nation.

Exacerbating the crisis, was America's support for two countries, Rwanda and Uganda, who were more than eager to jump in and line their pockets as well. Note that the U.S. was a major factor in Paul Kagame's rise to power.

Corporate purchasers of conflict or blood minerals were key to arming and feeding all the militias and to foreign countries that employed armies in the Congo. They were the life-blood of these militias.

As well, standing silently as either a nation or as a member of the United Nations while such horrors were destroying individuals, families and communities is tacitly offering support for the worst humanitarian disaster since World War 11.

CHAPTER 2

Somalia

After I watched an interview with a ten year-old Somalia boy in 2011, I began to understand the horror of living in Somalia and the terror besetting the population. He was asked why he was wandering around the streets of Mogadishu with an AK-47 instead of attending school to which he responded that he had to live and to search for food. Arms were awash in Somalia and poverty was ubiquitous forcing many people to rob others at gun point in order to survive.

War and exploitation both domestically and externally has raged since independence for which the U.S. bears significant complicity. Somalia was ruled either by a dictator or the absence of a central authority from 1977 to the present triggering atrocities, starvation and danger from various militias, warlords and rapacious Western and African countries.

During the scramble for Africa in the nineteenth century, the Somali people were carved up into different territories to meet the needs of the colonial powers. Somalia, Djibouti, Kenya and Ethiopia were populated with Somali people. This arbitrary and selfish division of the Somali people had dire consequences a century later.

Somalia became independent in 1960 and unification of the Somali people became a major driving force. From the outset, Somalia refused to accept its European-constructed borders and supported Somalia insurgents in the Ogaden region of Ethiopia. In 1963, the Soviet Union offered to establish an army of 10,000 men together with a small air force in Somalia. In the first of many wars between Somalia and Ethiopia over the Ogaden region, Ethiopia was victorious in a matter of days.

In 1967, Muhammad Haji Aribham Egal became Prime Minister but his tenure was cut short when the president was assassinated and the government fell victim to a military coup led by the Supreme Revolutionary Council (SRC) whose leader was Major General Mohamed Siyaad Barre. He immediately dissolved Parliament, the Supreme Court and the constitution. Barre's government established a large-scale public works program, implemented a literacy campaign and embarked on a campaign to nationalize industries.

Barre decided to disband the SRC and instead created the Somali Revolutionary Socialist Party. He then accepted a large number of Soviet advisors in government ministries and agencies while proclaiming Somalia a Marxist state. In 1972, as a Soviet satellite, Barre received increased military aid from the Soviet Union and built an army with 37,000 men and a modern air force with jet fighters.

With his new military prowess, Barre committed regular Somali forces to support the insurgents in the Ogaden region in Ethiopia and won possession of most of the territory within two months.

Unexpectedly, a massive Soviet intervention consisting of 20,000 Cuban forces and several thousand Soviet experts rushed to the aid of Ethiopia's communist Derg regime and by March 1978, the Somali troops were driven out of the Ogaden region. Abandoned by the Soviets, Barre sought support from the Soviet's arch-rival, the United States, which had been courting the Somali government for a number of years.

Due to the clannish nature of the Somali people, there was the ever-present danger that some of the clans would turn against Barre. Defeat in the Ogaden region reverberated throughout Somalia and leaders of the Majerteyn clan unsuccessfully attempted to overthrow Barre. They subsequently fled to Ethiopia where they launched a guerrilla war against Somalia. Another guerrilla war was initiated against Barre by the Somali National Movement (SNM), a northern group who had the support of Ethiopia.

By 1980, Barre's moral authority had virtually evaporated and the authority of his government was practically non-existent. The government became increasingly totalitarian in order to crush resistance and opposition to his rule.

Nevertheless, the United States negotiated an arms deal with Barre which granted Americans access to Somali bases. Another advantage of maintaining a close relationship with Barre was Somalia's strategic location bordering on the Red Sea. Bases in Somalia would provide an excellent platform to launch interventions in the Middle East.

Ethiopia greatly exacerbated Barre's troubles by supporting various resistance movements inside Somalia such as the Somalia Salvation Democratic Front (SSDF), United Somalia Congress (USC), Somalia National Movement (SNM) and the Somalia Patriotic Front (SPF) and political movements such as the Somalia Democratic Movement (SDM), the Somalia Democratic Alliance (SDA) and the Somali Manifesto Group (SMG).

Barre prohibited groups of more than four people from gathering in public in Mogadishu, fuel shortages caused long lines of cars at petroleum stations and the price of food was rising rapidly further inciting unrest. Barre's anti-Soviet posture ensured that western nations would continue to support him, in particular the United States, who gave him $80 million worth of aid, half of which were in military supplies. (Metz, H., C. Somalia: A Country Study. Federal Research Division: Library of Congress. May 1992)

This is another example of the United States and other Western countries propping up a government for their own political advantage despite the corruption and brutality of the recipient. Maintaining Barre in power was clearly not in the interest of the Somali people and prolonged their suffering under his rule. Human Rights Watch claims that Barre killed 50,000 civilians and displaced 500,000.

When Barre attempted to cut his losses by negotiating a deal with Ethiopia calling for both sides to abstain from supporting opposition groups in each other's countries, Barre aroused even more resentment from the Somali people who felt that he was betraying them. As a result, there was a rapid upsurge in fighting in northern Somalia during which SNM rebels were able to capture several towns in northern Somalia including the regional capital, Hargeisa. In response, Barre's air force repeatedly bombed the town forcing western countries to finally withdraw their support. Without Western support, Somalia disintegrated into an aggregation of rival fiefdoms ruled by local clan leaders all with their own stockpile of arms. Reflecting the breakdown of the population, the army splintered into rival factions. The result was a country besieged by lawlessness.

By 1990, Barre's control barely reached the outskirts of Mogadishu where, even there, his authority was challenged by his main rival, General Muhammed Farah Aideed, military leader of the USC, who had been imprisoned by Barre without a trial. His militia was based on a sub-clan of the Hawiye.

At this point, Barre's authority had completely collapsed creating the opportunity for Aideed's militia, backed by Derg's regime in Ethiopia, to drive Barre out of Mogadishu in January 1991. He fled southward with a convoy of gold bars and foreign currency, most of it stolen.

Barre's departure provoked a war among various clans for control over Somalia which persevered for many years leaving a vacuum in place of a central government. Violence, lack of development and constant warfare were Barre's departing gift to the people of Somalia.

In January 1991, while Aideed was preoccupied with chasing Barre's forces, the Somali Manifesto Group (SMG) selected Ali Mahdi Muhammad as interim president until a conference of all stakeholders were to meet in Djibouti the following month to select a national leader. Aideed, leader of the United Somali Congress

(USC), Abdirahman Ahmed Ali Tuur, leader of the Somali National Leader Movement (SNL) and Colonel Ahmed Omar Jess, leader of the Somali Patriotic Movement (SPM) leader refused to recognize Mahdi as leader.

Rivalry between Mahdi's and Aideed's forces divided the capital into two armed camps and plunged it into a conflict for control of Mogadishu which left 14,000 dead and 40,000 wounded. As a result of the conflict, Mahdi's militias controlled the north and Aideed's militias controlled the south, leaving in its wake a city reduced to rubble. Outside of Mogadishu, clans claimed control of their local territory partitioning Somalia into an aggregation of regions controlled by rival clans. Civil strife disrupted agriculture and food distribution in southern Somalia resulting in a famine that claimed 300,000 victims.

Somalia's plight attracted the attention of UN Secretary-General Boutros Boutros-Ghali who had a vision for a new United Nation's agenda which called for a more active role for the UN called *An Agenda for Peace*. At this point, only the International Committee of the Red Cross was prepared to risk the dangers of a relief effort.

A window of opportunity for UN intervention opened up for the UN in March 1992 when Aideed and Mahdi agreed to a ceasefire. On April 24 1992, the UN Security Council authorized a United Nations operation in Somalia (UNOSOM) to be headed by Mohamed Sahnoun, which called for the immediate deployment of observers and a security force to be arranged in consultation with the parties in Mogadishu.

Aideed was deeply suspicious of UN motives and it wasn't until August that he agreed to the deployment of a security force consisting of 500 Pakistani soldiers. Meanwhile, the streets of Mogadishu were ruled by roving militias who controlled access to the port and international airport and held relief supplies for ransom.

Notwithstanding the strife and chaos in the capital, Sahnoun endeavoured to apply his soft approach by attempting to gain the trust of the militia leaders. Sahnoun's efforts to carry out his mandate were burdened with bureaucratic bickering, endless delays, a shortage of resources and a deaf ear at UN headquarters. Boutros-Ghali abruptly dismissed him on the basis that he was making high-profile complaints. He was replaced by Ismat Kittani, an Iraqi diplomat, who was confrontational compared to the soft approach of his predecessor.

International aid agencies, who were witnessing the disaster first-hand, mounted a drumbeat for more aggressive action by the United Nations. They argued that the absence of a central authority, wanton destruction and the difficulties in distributing aid due the random violence demanded the presence of a contingent of UN troops to address these problems.

George H. W. Bush, still celebrating his ostensible victory in Iraq which was anything but a victory for the Iraqis, was now ready to prove that he could undertake a real humanitarian intervention by playing a central role in a Somalia mission with humanitarian objectives and offered to lead UN forces to ensure the distribution of aid.

On December 3 1992, the UN passed resolution 794 sanctioning an American-led multinational force - UNITAF - code-named Operation Restore Hope, which was mandated to create a protected environment for humanitarian operations. UNITAF was led by the U.S. military with a contingent of 37,000 troops from a number of nations, 28,000 of whom were Americans.

A disagreement flared up between Bush and Boutros-Ghali about whether or not to disarm the rebels. Boutros-Ghali believed it was essential to disarm the militias while the pentagon was adamantly opposed to the idea in order to avoid further casualties. Bush insisted that the U.S. contribution be no more than a "limited Salvation Army role."

In a stage-managed piece of theatre meant to have the maximum impact in the United States, U.S. troops landed in Somalia on December 9. Marine Corps and Navy special operations personnel along with 1,300 marines arrived by helicopter at the Mogadishu airport and were greeted by the blazing lights of media crews.

By 1993, the worst of the famine had already passed calling into question the real U.S. motives for U.S. participation in UNITAF. In addition to the strategic motives for securing Somalia as a client-state was the motive of exploring for oil by American companies such as Amoco, Chevron and Conoco. There was even a close relationship between Conoco and American forces in Somalia whose headquarters were located in Conoco's Mogadishu headquarters.

As well, Somalis recognized that the U.S. forces who were allegedly there to offer support for aid distribution were representative of the same forces which had propped up the dictator who was largely responsible for the current crises in Somalia.

As U.S. casualties mounted, an increasing number of Somalis found themselves under attack. Clinton's words on Somalia, according to George Stephanopoulos were:

> We're not inflicting pain on these fuckers. When people kill us, they should be killed in greater numbers. I believe in killing people who try to hurt you. And I can't believe we're being pushed around by these pricks. (George Stephanopoulos, *All Too Human*, March 2001, Back Bay Books)

In a misguided attempt to aim for zero casualties, Aideed and Mahdi were almost treated as partners by allowing them to keep their arsenals and designated compounds. There was no real effort to destroy arm caches thus creating the perception among Somalis that the U.S. was not interested in ensuring a peaceful environment for distribution of aid but to leave Somalia with no casualties.

Although UNITAF saved lives, its success was relatively limited. According to the refugee policy group:

> 240,000 is the estimate for excess mortality due to fighting and famine, and 154,000 represents the number thereof who could most readily have been saved through timely and effective action. About 10 – 25,000 [were saved] during the subsequent UNITAF intervention period. (Refugee Policy Group, *Refugee Policy Group, Hope Restored? Humanitarian Aid in Somalia 1990 – 1994,* Washington DC, 1994, p. 5)

Additionally, aid officials in Somalia reported that 90% of the rural population were suffering from lack of food. (ibid)

One positive achievement of UNITAF was that its presence encouraged the warring warlords to arrange a meeting to be held in Addis Ababa in March 1993 for the purpose of arranging a ceasefire and to begin a representative political process. The conference communique agreed to a National Transitional Government, drafting of a constitution and setting up a committee for disarmament.

Although Aideed had signed the agreement, he was very suspicious of the UN and U.S. motives and believed in the self-fulfilling prophecy that they were targeting him and favouring the other warlords. He unleashed a verbal onslaught of criticism against both UN and U.S officials and refused to implement the terms agreed to in Addis Ababa. Since both UN and U.S. officials concluded that Aideed would settle for nothing less than absolute power, they believed he needed to be brought under control. Robert Gosende, the new U.S. special envoy, voiced the opinion that Aideed should be arrested for non-cooperation with the 1993 Addis agreement.

As it was becoming clear that the only solution to the conflicts among warlords in Somalia was to disarm all the militias, the United Nations authorized a more aggressive mission based on Chapter VII of the UN Charter to be named UNOSOM II. A Chapter VII mission authorizes the use of force "for the maintenance of international peace and security" (Article 48, Chapter VII). According to the United Nations:

The mandate of UNOSOM II was to take appropriate action, including enforcement measures, to establish throughout Somalia a secure environment for humanitarian assistance. To that end, UNOSOM II was to complete, through disarmament and reconciliation, the task begun by UNITAF for the restoration of peace, stability, law and order. (United Nations, *United Nations Operation in Somalia, Somalia – UNSCOM II, Mandate*, 1993)

The mandate in Resolution 814 authorized UNOSOM II to be involved in:

- monitoring that all factions continued to respect the cessation of hostilities and other agreements to which they had consented;
- preventing any resumption of violence and, if necessary, taking appropriate action;
- maintaining control of the heavy weapons of the organized factions which would be brought under international control. (United Nations, *Resolution 814*, 1993)

Resolution 814 called for the discharge of very ambitious responsibilities including the establishment of a new government, a new police force, a new justice system and building a strong economy. Its mandate called for the creation of a peaceful environment for the distribution of aid and peace enforcement, necessitating disarmament of the militias.

A new multinational force was created consisting of 20,000 peacekeeping troops, 8,000 logistical staff and 3,000 civilian personnel from 23 nations.

The U.S. was not neutral and had a powerful motive for eliminating Aideed. Chevron and Conoco were exploring for oil in Somalia and had established a close relationship with American armed forces whose headquarters were located in Conoco's Mogadishu headquarters. America envoy, Robert Oakley, had close relations with Conoco which provided military intelligence to American forces. President W. Bush wrote a letter to Dino Nicandros, President of Continental Oil Company, in which he offered his gratitude for their assistance in Somalia by stating that, "I am writing to express my deep appreciation to Conoco and to its representative in Somalia, Raymond Marchand, who made it possible for Ambassador Oakley and his team to work effectively." (Bush, G., W. *Letter to Dino Nicandros.* The Conoco-Somalia Declassification Project. December 16, 1992).

When UNITAF was still operational, UNITAF troops had allowed an Aideed rival militia to occupy the town of Kismayu while ousting a pro-Aideed militia, the seed of suspicion that the UN was targeting Aideed's militia was firmly planted. The new UN force assembled in Mogadishu, further convincing Aideed that its mandate was directed only at his militia rather than any other.

To demonstrate his anger at the UN, he had sent troops into the street to riot and to prepare to resist any further moves by the UN to further weaken his power. Since U.S. officials already believed that Aideed aspired to gain complete control of Somalia, a clash between Aideed and UNOSOM II became virtually inevitable.

On June 3, General Montgomery, deputy commander of UNOSOM forces, sent a letter to Admiral Howe, overall commander of

UNOSOM, announcing a weapons inspection of Aideed's weapons sites as agreed to in the Addis Ababi accords. After Howe consulted with his chief political advisor, April Glaspie, about the inspection, the letter was delivered to a SNA official who read it and proclaimed "this means war". When Howe was informed about the delivery of the inspection, the words "this means war" were omitted.

U.S. decision to inspect Aideed's weapons sites first was a tragic error in judgement which ignored the underlying purpose of any UN mission to maintain international peace and security. It was a very provocative act given the history between the American's UNOSOM staff and Aideed. Adding fuel to the fire that was already blazing was clearly not in the interest in maintaining peace. Furthermore, not informing Howe of the response by Aideed's official, was foolish, almost guaranteeing that a conflict would erupt.

A further mistake by UNOSOM was to choose an Aideed site that also housed his radio station. Aideed's men were now suspicious that the real purpose of the mission was to destroy his radio station. Given the circumstances to date, it is not an unreasonable conclusion. An Aideed official warned UNSCOM that "This is unacceptable. This means war". U.S. commanders received the warning but failed to inform the Pakistani troops who were assigned to carry out the inspection.

The series of errors on the part of the Americans arouses suspicions that they were actually targeting Aideed. Failing to inform the Pakistani contingent was bound to lead to trouble. Aideed was not really different than the other warlords yet he was singled out and the conflict that resulted from the series of deliberate mistakes was absolutely avoidable. United Nation's principles call for negotiation, compromise, diplomacy and avoiding conflict which were not applied in American's stance vis-à-vis Aideed.

When the inspection was carried out on June 5, 1993, an angry crowd waited outside to protest the inspection of Aideed's radio station. As the Pakistani soldiers emerged, they were attacked and shots were fired. Twenty-four soldiers were killed and many more injured by the crowd as UNOSOM soldiers tried to calm a crowd at a food distribution centre.

Washington's response was spontaneous combustion causing them to change the mission in Somalia but without any investigation first of the Aideed incidents. The assumption was that Aideed was responsible for all the incidents and that he should be arrested immediately. America's previous actions and its reaction to the three incidents confirm that they had targeted Aideed from the very beginning. Their plan was to shoot first and ask questions later.

With pressure from the United States, the Security Council hastily passed resolution 837 authorizing Boutros-Ghali to take "all necessary measures against all those responsible for the armed attacks...to secure the investigation of their actions and their arrest and detention for prosecution, trail and punishment." Resolution 837 was a declaration of war. Clearly, the handling of UNOSOM's relationship with Aideed was not in the spirit of the UN Charter.

In the Charter it states that:

- to ensure, by the acceptance of principles and the institution of methods, that armed force shall not be used, save in the common interest; (preamble)

- To maintain international peace and security, and to that end: to take effective collective measures for the prevention and removal of threats to the peace, and for the suppression of acts of aggression or other breaches of the peace, and to bring about by peaceful means, and in conformity with the principles of justice and international law, adjustment or settlement of international disputes or situations which might lead to a breach of the peace; (Article 1)

- The parties to any dispute, the continuance of which is likely to endanger the maintenance of international peace and security, shall, first of all, seek a solution by negotiation, enquiry, mediation, conciliation, arbitration, judicial settlement, resort to regional agencies or arrangements, or other peaceful means of their own choice. (Article 33)

These articles declare that force should be a very last resort and all other means must be exhausted first. America's approach to Aideed was provocative and threatening and no channels of communication were established to resolve misunderstandings of intentions or actions.

The cost of America's failure to act in the spirit of the UN Charter and the United Nation's hasty concession to U.S. pressure led to a four month war. Immediately, the U.S. converted its old embassy into a war centre surrounded by razor wire and sandbagged bunkers.

Admiral Howe was situated in a reinforced underground bunker which served as his headquarters. He was a man on a mission and according to John Drysdale, a UNOSOM advisor: "He gave the impression of a crusader with a burning passion to right the wrongs, as he perceived them, of one man, Aideed, at whatever the cost." It is unfortunate that he didn't have the same passion for trying to resolve the problem without the use of force.

America immediately embarked on a bombing campaign to destroy Radio Aideed, weapon sites, garages and houses. As well, Americans launched a manhunt for Aideed but he managed to stay one step ahead of them although some of his supporters were found and jailed.

On July 11, a Somali informer revealed the location where Aideed planned to hold a meeting but, in fact, the purpose of the meeting was to enable a group of intellectuals, businessmen and clan elders to discuss proposals to open a dialogue with UNOSOM. Some of those at the meeting had met Howe two days earlier to begin the process of opening a dialogue. Rather than grab the opportunity to avoid any further damage wrought by a war, U.S. commanders leaped on the chance to kill Aideed via an air strike. The plan was for the informer to leave the meeting at the appropriate time to give a signal to a communications helicopter which in turn would call in a strike force of three helicopters. Once the informer left the meeting, three Cobra helicopters moved in, firing missiles at the building which was virtually obliterated. U.S. marines moved in to finish off any survivors. No warning was given and no attempt to was given to the people in the building to surrender. This action by U.S. forces acting on behalf of a UN peacekeeping mission is a violation of everything for which the United Nations stands and violates every principle of peacekeeping, again confirming that the U.S. real objective was to kill Aideed. Aideed had never been in the building.

Surprisingly, Admiral Howe declared the strike a victory and boasted that:

> We hit a key military planning cell of key Aideed advisers. This is where they have done their plotting for terrorist attacks. We knew what we were hitting. It was well planned. (Martin Meredith, *The Fate of Africa: A History of Fifty Years of Independence*, New York: Public Affairs, 2005)

A number of UN officials expressed their horror at an operation that was clearly a case of murder. Ann Wright, an American lawyer who headed UNOSOM's justice division, resigned in protest.

Howe was unaffected by the incident and so frustrated that Aideed had escaped his clutches that he requested reinforcements. A team of specialists were dispatched to Mogadishu consisting of 400 rangers and 130 Delta Force commandos.

Their next attempt to capture or kill Aideed was even more embarrassing when the Americans were tipped off that Aideed was hiding at a house in the Lig Lagato compound where they abseiled onto the roof, burst into the building with guns ablazing and arrested nine people. Residents of the building included a representative of the United Nations development programme, three international staff members and a senior Egyptian lady. In another disastrous effort, an assault force entered the residence of a Somali general who was being trained by the UN and arrested him along with 38 other residents. Additional raids were equally embarrassing.

All these futile attempts to capture or kill Aideed began to prompt questions from Washington officials about the wisdom of the strategy adopted by American forces in UNOSOM to achieve its objectives. A Senate resolution was passed requiring the President to seek authorization from Congress by November 15 if he wanted to continue to deploy troops in Somalia.

Before November 15 arrived, U.S. forces committed a fatal blunder that ended their so-called humanitarian mission. On October 3, there were reports that two of Aideed's closest associates were meeting in a house on Hawlwadig Road in Mogadishu. A strike force of sixteen helicopters, eight carrying troops, and a ground convoy of 12 vehicles headed for the target three miles away. The strike force consisted of 160 Rangers and Delta Force operators.

A raid into the centre of Aideed's stronghold was certainly a foolish decision as thousands poured out into the streets, most of whom were armed, to greet the strike force with a counterattack on the U.S. forces and helicopters. Helicopters and ground forces suddenly became engulfed in a firefight with angry Somalis. American soldiers entered the targeted house and arrested 24 Somalis including Aideed's close associates.

Somalis fought back and shot down two Black Hawk helicopters and damaged two others. A convoy carrying the prisoners weaved its way through the streets of Mogadishu in a desperate attempt to avoid further clashes with Somalis. When the convoy lost its way, a rescue convoy attempted to reach the lost convoy but ran into a hail storm of gunfire and barricades resulting in the death or injury of 100 Americans. Eighteen soldiers died and 82 were injured but after the Americans managed to escape, two American bodies were dragged through the streets of Mogadishu as a celebration of victory over the United States. The battered corpses of the two dead Americans being dragged through the streets of Mogadishu was a made-for-TV moment which was shown repeatedly on American television.

This humiliating and embarrassing moment compelled President Clinton to call off the hunt for Aideed and withdraw all American forces from Somalia by March 13, 1994. Without the American forces, UNOSOM could not survive and its withdrawal ended in March 1995.

The original purpose of the UN involvement in Somalia to ensure the delivery of food aid was mutated by the Americans into a mission to hunt down one particular warlord with whom they didn't believe they could do business. American interests superseded humanitarian objectives.

After the Americans and UN pulled out of Somalia, the people of Somalia suffered through nine years without a strong, widely supported central government. As well, there was constant warfare among the clans with little or no economic development.

Aideed declared himself president in June 1995, but his government was not officially recognized internationally, limiting aid and loans from other nations and international institutions. During his brief tenure, clans fiercely fought for control of Mogadishu. On July 24,

1996, Aideed and his militia fought a brutal battle with warlords and the militia of Mahdi during which Aideed was wounded, succumbing to a heart attack on August 1.

His son, Hussein Mohamed Aideed was selected by the Somali National Alliance to become the new president. Battles between the warlords continued unabated, the result of which was an absence of a real central government.

From November 1996 to January 1997, to put an end to the strife, warlords met to discuss and put an end to the divisiveness of their internecine battles and to create a 41-member National Salvation Council (NSC) charged with the responsibility of organizing a transitional government. The conference was boycotted by Hussein and thus rendered meaningless.

In December 1997, another reconciliation meeting was held in Cairo where 28 warlords signed the Cairo Declaration. This time both Mahdi and Hussein were in attendance and signed the document.

Hussein, in accordance with the terms of the Declaration, relinquished his disputed title of president of Somalia. On March 30, 1998, Mahdi and Hussein formed a peace plan in which they both agreed to share power. The declaration was fatally flawed in that it created a 13-person Council of Presidents but failed to create a national leader. Without a central authority, there was no one person to lead the government with programs and no one to establish peace and order.

A series of meetings of Somali leaders were held in Arta, Dijbouti from April 20, 2000 to May 5, 2000 but in contrast to previous conferences, the Arta Conference included extensive participation by civic leaders, intellectuals, clan and religious leaders and members of the business community. It concluded with the formation of the Transitional National Government (TNG).

Opposing the TNG was a rival pan-Somalia government movement known as the Somalia Reconciliation and Restoration Council (SRRC), established in 2001, consisting of warlords from different regions of the country including Puntland who were not invited to the Arta Conference. These factional warlords effectively resisted and prevented the TNG from expanding and gaining control over all of Mogadishu.

The TNG consisted of a 245 member Transitional National Assembly reflecting the strength of the various clans participating and it elected Abdiqassim Salad Hassan as president of Somalia. Its mandate was to function as the government until August 2003 at which time a constitutional conference would be held leading up to elections.

Although a central government was in place, it exercised very little power in Somalia due to the perception among Somalis that it was illegal and unrepresentative. It did win the support of militia factions controlling Mogadishu, Puntland, Somaliland, and the Rahanwayn Resistance Army (RRA) - established as an autonomous region in 1999 by clans in the Bay and Bakool districts. In addition, the TNG was criticized for its domination by one clan, the Hawiye clan-family and much of the business community. Even worse, it was internally divided.

Its lack of legitimacy prevented it from exercising control over Mogadishu and it was unable to even collect taxes, control the ports, or attract the level of foreign assistance that was desperately needed. On the other hand, the SRRC had the support of numerous political parties, clan militias and other groups opposed to the TNG. Abdulaahi Yusuf Ahmed, the leader of the Puntland, was the leader of the SRRC. Paradoxically, the clans in the SRRC had been at war with each other but were drawn together because of their common opposition to the TNG. It is important to note that the SRRG enjoyed Ethiopian patronage.

By 2002, lacking the necessary support internally and without recognition by foreign powers, it was clear that the TNG was not the solution to Somalia's problems. To address the deficiency of a strong central government, the International Agency for Development (IAFD), a regional organization in the Horn of Africa, launched a National Reconciliation Conference in Mbagathi, Kenya, inviting both the now defunct TNG and the SRRC. Tortuous and protracted, the talks had resulted in some progress by 2004 in which a 275-member transitional parliament had been established under the Transitional Federal Government (TFG) which was going to operate out of Nairobi, Kenya. October 14, 2004, the TFG elected Abdulaahi Yusuf Ahmed as interim president who appointed Ali Muhammad as his Prime Minister. A Transitional National Charter was drawn up at the meetings infusing the TFG with legitimacy. It was to be submitted to the people of Somalia for a referendum.

Problems plagued the TFG from the start. President Yusuf, an archetypal warlord, was a problematic choice given his focus in the past on military action while governance and political issues occupied second place. For example, he attempted to control Puntland by the use of force, which had been seeking independence for many years. He had also established ties to Ethiopia and was considered a proxy for that country in the context of the struggle over the Ogaden region in Ethiopia.

The December 12 deadline for relocation from Nairobi to Mogadishu had passed and by 2005 the new government had yet to be installed. On February 2006, the parliament first met inside Somalia in the city of Baidoa, 260 kilometers northwest of Mogadishu.

While warlords were enmeshed in constant warfare with each other, unable to reach any common ground for a cohesive, representative government, another group was moving in the opposite direction in 1994 by becoming more cohesive and united in their struggle to form the government in Somalia.

Lack of a central authority, constant warfare and lawlessness induced a number of Islamic judges to form sharia-based courts to serve as the judicial system in Somalia. The judges in these courts were not adherents to any particular school of Islamic law, or in other words, were not extreme in any sense and were only devoted to maintaining law and order. These courts assumed the responsibility to halt robberies and drug-dealing and fill the void created by the lack of a judicial system. Eventually the courts, known as the Islamic Union of Courts (ICU), also acted as the local police force to fill that void as well. They were funded by fees paid by litigants and local businesses to reduce crime.

Since social services were absent due to the lack of a central government, these courts began to provide services in the fields of health care and education. Since Somalia was almost entirely Muslim and desperately needed the services provided by the courts, they became widely popular.

Islamic clerics from the Abgal sub-clan of the Hawiye (Somalia's largest and most powerful clan) established the first court in 1994 in north Mogadishu. As the number of courts grew, they recognized the value in working together through a joint committee to promote security. By uniting together, the courts could co-ordinate the policies they practiced in their individual courts. This move was initiated by four of the courts who formed a committee to co-ordinate their affairs, to exchange criminals from different clans and to integrate security forces. Supporters of the Islamic courts and other institutions united to form the ICUP, an armed militia. In 1999, the Islamic courts began to assert its authority, armed and financed by the Eritrean government, and took control of the main market in Mogadishu, capturing the road from Mogadishu to Afgoi.

In 2000, the courts formally united and became the Union of Islamic Courts (UIC) to consolidate their resources and power although the ICU remained firmly entrenched in the Hawiye clan. There were some internal strife between the Islamic courts in the South and the North but by the end of 2004, they worked together and elected Sheikh Sharif Ahmed as Chairman. As the courts began to gain strength, they became a threat to the warlords who controlled much of Mogadishu and they created the Alliance for the Restoration of Peace and Counter-Terrorism (ARPCT) to counter the strength of the ICUP.

As the UIC gained cohesion, strength and presence and began to encroach upon the authority of the warlords within the TFG, clashes became inevitable. Fighting in the capital escalated claiming 300 lives in its wake.

Fearing an Islamic government and as part of the American war on terror, the United States embarked on a campaign to support warlords and to deploy CIA and JSOC teams on a regular basis in Somalia. According to Armytimes, a newspaper serving active and retired military personnel, "Starting in 2003, small teams of U.S. operatives would...embark on one of the most dangerous missions conducted by U.S. personnel in Somalia....The teams combined CIA case officers and "shooters" from a secretive special operations unit sometimes called Task Force Orange...The operatives set out to build relationships with the warlords who held sway in Somalia for the previous 12 years."(Naylor, S., D. Clandestine Somalia missions yield AQ targets). Armytimes, November 14, 2011. P. 1-2) Their base was Camp Lemonnier in Djibouti where the U.S. eventually established AFRICOM.

In addition, the U.S. was paying between $100,000 and $150,000 per month to warlords to capture suspected members of al Qaeda. CIA operatives were also paying trusted Somalis "$1000 to $2000 a month to enter southern Somalia and report what they observed." (Naylor, S., D. Clandestine Somalia missions yield AQ targets). Armytimes, November 14, 2011. P. 8)

Rather than expend resources to finance warlords' dubious missions to capture the few radicals seeking refuge in Somalia, a more effective strategy would have been to disarm the warlords who were relentlessly destabilizing the country. According to Jeremy Scahill, "Washington directly supported an expansion of their (warlords) power and, in the process, caused a radical backlash, opening the doors wide for al Qaeda to step in." (Scahill, J. *Dirty Wars: The World is a Battlefield.* New York: Nation Books, 2013. P. 121) Warlords supported by Washington engaged in ruthless tactics to gain control of territory using the war on terrorism to cover their activities. Jeremy Scahill observed that, "American activities [in Somalia]…had transformed into death squads roaming Somalia, killing with impunity and widely viewed as being directly supported and encouraged by the United States." (Scahill, J. Dirty Wars: The World is a Battlefield. New York: Nation Books, 2013. P. 192)

During 2005, members of the UIC were victims of a number of unexplained disappearances leading to the conclusion that the U.S. was targeting their members and, in particular, targeting militia commanders of some of the courts. These men did not have a religious background but were the "driving force behind the implementation of court jurisdictions." "(Cedric Barnes and Harun Hassan, *The Rise and Fall Islamic Courts of Mogadishu's Islamic Courts*, Chatham House, April 2007) According to Omar Jamal, executive director of the Somalia Advocacy Center in St Paul, Minnesota, "You have all this illegal kidnapping going on, by taking people from Mogadishu city to the [U.S.] base for interrogations." (Omar Jamal, *Is the U.S. Government Fueling Civil War in Somalia,* Democracy Now, May 18 2006)

United States was one of the main supporters of the ARPCT because they were determined to ensure that an Islamic group did not form a government in Somalia. Washington automatically assumed that an Islamic government somehow involved terrorists or opened the door to terrorism in the country. President George W. Bush expressed his fear of terrorism taking root under an UIC government when he explained that, "[Our] first concern, of course, would be to make sure that Somalia does not become an al-Qaida safe haven, doesn't become a place from which terrorists plot and plan." (PBS NEWSHOUR, *Islamic Control of Mogadishu Raises Concern of Extremist Future for Somalia,* June 8 2006)

State Department spokesman, Sean McCormack, voiced a similar opinion stating that, "We certainly want to work with people in Somalia who are interested in combatting terrorism. We do have concerns about the presence of al-Qaeda in Somalia." (Saeed Shabazz, *UN trying to clarify problems in Somalia*, World News, June 29 2006)

In an attempt to minimize the risk of an Islamic government, American's set up bases around Somalia. According to Omar Jamal:

> It's really a fact that the State Department has that that they are working with responsible individuals in fighting terrorism in Mogadishu city, which means funding criminal warlords. It's very obvious that it is contributing to the instability of the country. The U.S. government is there by having aircrafts all around the Indian Ocean and have a base at Djibouti, the Horn of Africa and a terrorism task force. (Omar Jamal, *Is the U.S. Government Fueling Civil War in Somalia*, Democracy Now, May 18 2006)

U.S. Secretary-General of the UN, Kofi Annan, warned the U.S. about the dangers of supporting warlords in Somalia. According to Annan, "It was wrong for the United States government to support warlords in Somalia. I would not have recommended to the UN

Security Council to support warlords." (Saeed Shabazz, *UN trying to clarify problems in Somalia*, World News, June 29 2006)

Painting all Islamic organizations or governments with the same brush blinded Washington to the nuances to be found within any race, nationality, ethnicity or tribe. According to some experts on Somalia, "Analysts watching developments in Somalia, and Somalia expatriates, claim the U.S. fear of a fundamentalist regime in a country known for its moderate religious beliefs is unfounded." (ibid)

On the other hand, lacking a central government and complete destabilization of the country is an open invitation to terrorists to move in and establish bases. John Prendergast states that:

> The president of a neighboring country told me recently that the 'governance vacuum' is growing larger, with very negative implications for Somalia. It increases the potential for international terrorists to use the structures that are filling the vacuum for safe haven and logistical purposes. (John Prendergast, *U.S. Counterterrorism Policy is Empowering Islamist Militias*, Washington Post, June 7 2006)

War between the UIC and the warlords temporarily abated on June 6 2006, after a two month long battle when the UIC took over Mogadishu. When the warlords fled the city with most of them seeking refuge in Jowhar where they were defeated on June 14 2006, the UIC were virtually in control of most of the country.

In expanding their control throughout Somalia, the UIC restored peace and security inspiring a mood of optimism among the people of Somalia for the first time in approximately 15 years.

UIC's stabilization success resulted in reopening the airport, safe schools and the meeting of basic needs. Crimes of the warlords such as kidnapping, corruption and extortion were no longer tolerated. For their brief time in office, they unified most of the country and restored a sense of nationhood.

The Centre for Strategic and International Studies pointed out that, "The near-constant warfare stopped, crime plummeted, and businesses reopened, gaining the ICU a great deal of support among Mogadishu residents." (PBS NEWSHOUR. Islamic Control of Mogadishu Raises Concerns of Extremist Future for Somalia. June 8, 2006) It is important to note that the courts were not radical and did not have connections to al Qaeda. Their work concentrated on health care, education, peace and security. According to The Royal Institute of International Affairs, a British sister group to the Council on Foreign Relations, "The Courts achieved the unthinkable, uniting Mogadishu for the first time, and re-establishing peace and security." (Barnes, c. and Hassan, H.) *The Rise and Fall of Mogadishu's Islamic Courts*. Chatham House: April, 2007) In addition, The International Refugee Rights Initiative affirmed that, "The Islamic Courts were...able to introduce a measure of peace and security in Southern Somalia...The security was welcomed by much of the local population." (International Refugee Rights Initiative). *Somalia: A Humanitarian Crisis Disregarded*. Refugee Rights News, Volume 4, Issue 4. June 2008)

It is probable that you will travel in the wrong direction if you are wearing blinkers. Thus the United States decided, all evidence to the contrary, that the UIC was a threat simply because they were

Islamic and Bush's administration was determined to remove them from office.

Jendayi E. Frazier, U.S. Assistant Secretary of State, led the charge against the UIC by planning a military solution to the ostensible problem in Somalia, the UIC. She colluded with Meles Zenawi, leader of the minority regime in Ethiopia, to invade Somalia by the end of 2006. Yet again, the U.S. was employing a proxy to do its dirty work to save American casualties and avoid condemnation by world opinion, opinion at home and international organizations such as the UN.

America's role in first convincing Ethiopia to invade Somalia and its support for such an invasion was made clear in the following cable from Azouz Ennifar, Acting Special Representative of the Secretary-General for the United Nations Mission in Ethiopia and Eritrea (UNMEE) in Addis Ababa, to Jean-Marie Guehenno, UN Under Secretary-General for Peacekeeping Operations, in New York; the subject of which was a "Meeting with US Assistant Secretary of State for African Affairs (Jendasyl Frazer). Present at the meeting were the following officials: Dr. Frazer, Rear Admiral, US Navy, Richard W. Hunt, Commander Combined Joint Task Force Horn of Africa, Ambassador Vikki Huddleston, U.S. Chargé d'Affaires in Addis Ababa, Colonel Richard Orth, the Military Attaché at the U.S. Embassy in Addis Ababa and Abdel Haireche, Force Commander. According to the cable:

> The US Assistant Secretary's visit to Addis Ababa and meetings with Prime Minister Meles and the presence of Rear Admiral Hunt at her side show Washington's growing concerns about the evolving situation in Somalia and the

Region. If in the past, the U.S. and Ethiopia had diverging views and strategies on the way forward in Somalia...the UIC's military achievements have definitely led to a rapprochement and to the potential development of a common approach to the problem. Any Ethiopian action in Somalia would have Washington's blessing. (WikiLeaks, *Meeting with..., Addis Ababa*, June 26, 2006, Release date: November 26, 2009)

Also revealed in the cable was an assessment of Ethiopia's military capability:

Ethiopia does not have enough force to sustain a march on Mogadishu, therefore it would need to pull elements from the 21 divisions in the north and along the Temporary Security Zone. The Rear Admiral expressed the view that the Ethiopian army could not sustain two fronts simultaneously, and inquired if UMEE had the capacity to monitor military preparations by the Ethiopian and Eritrean armies at the border. (ibid)

America's blessing, funding and intelligence were only part of the support offered to Ethiopia in its plan to invade and capture Somalia. A small number of U.S. Special Forces Troops accompanied Ethiopian and TFG forces after the collapse of the UIC to give military advice and assist in tracking Islamic guerrilla forces.

Ethiopian invasion of Somalia with U.S. support violated the UN Charter, Article 51, the African Union Charter and the invasion itself violated a number of international laws including the Geneva Conventions.

Furthermore, the U.S. was subjecting the people of Somalia to another war despite the fact the UIC had brought peace and stability to Somalia. Salim Lone, columnist for the Daily Nation in Kenya and former spokesperson for the UN mission in Iraq explains that, "In Somalia, clashes between U.S. backed-Ethiopian forces and fighters aligned with the Islamic Courts Union in the capital Mogadishu are being described as some of the heaviest fighting in the city's history." (Salim Lone, *The Most Lawless War in our Generation*, Democracy Now, April 27, 2007)

Subsequent to the Ethiopian invasion of Somalia, the UN attempted on several occasions to pass a resolution forcing Ethiopia to withdraw from Somalia but the United States used its veto power to defeat these resolutions. In the Review of African Political Economy, it was revealed that, "Meanwhile the U.S. and its allies blocked two attempts by the UN Security Council that called for immediate Ethiopian withdrawal." (Abdi Ismail Samatar, *Ethiopian Invasion of Somalia, US Warlordism and AU Shame*, Review of African Political Economy, Vol. 34 No. 11, March 2007)

The Ethiopian invasion was condemned by the United Nations for further destabilizing a country wracked for decades by conflict and the lack of a central government. When the UIC finally established a central government and law and order, Ethiopia and the U.S., driven by their own agenda, intervened and further destabilized the country. In the long run, the consequences of the invasion are also devastating due to the creation of a radical wing of the UIC that prolonged the conflict to this day.

War officially began on June 20, 2006, when U.S.-backed Ethiopian troops invaded Somalia to support the TFG who had stationed themselves in Baidoa. ICU forces that controlled the coastal areas of southern Somalia were attacked by the forces of the Ethiopian-backed TFG. TFG forces enjoyed several successes and on December 29 marched into Mogadishu relatively unopposed.

On February 20 2007, the United Nations adopted Resolution 1744 which created a Chapter VII mission to Somalia known as African Union Mission to Somalia (AMISOM) whose mandate was to support Transitional Government structures, implement a national security plan, train the Somali security forces, to secure a safe environment for the delivery of humanitarian aid and to support the Transitional Federal Government's forces in their battle against Al Shabaab (discussed below) militants. Its mandate has been renewed many times and is still present in Somalia today.

In January 2007, pursuant to their defeat in Mogadishu, UIC forces retreated to Ras Kamboni where they were pursued by Ethiopian and TFG forces. Since Ras Kamboni is at the southern tip of Somalia on the ocean and shares a border with Kenya, the U.S. enforced a naval blockade and border patrol, followed by airstrikes.

Another means of U.S. support for the TFG and Ethiopian forces involved the use of American bombers and an aircraft carrier group, the USS Dwight D. Eisenhower, anchored off the coast of Somalia. As is often the case when American forces rely on bombing, many innocent people become victims.

Sometimes, a small percentage of victims are terrorists. It is important to recognize that when the American government describes targets as terrorists, they are justifying their actions by lumping together a wide spectrum of people. Sometimes the victims are actually terrorists but sometimes they are insurgents or just plain innocent civilians. In addition, UIC insurgents have every right to fight back after losing power illegitimately against two foreign governments and a group, the TFG, who had been previously displaced from power.

For example, U.S. helicopter gunship attacks against suspected Islamic extremists near Afmadow on January 9, 2007, killed 31 civilians and two newlyweds according to witnesses. (Mohamed Olad Hassan, *Somalia officials says U.S. helicopter gunships...*, Associated Press, January 9 2007)

In another case, witnesses reported to the BBC that the town of Afmadow was also bombed on January 9 by U.S. helicopters and that the local MP announced the death toll at 27. (BBC, US *Somali air strikes 'kill many'*, January 9 2007)

In January 2007, the Ethiopian government claimed victory over the ICU which had been overpowered by the Ethiopian forces and the TFG both had been supported by American bombing, intelligence and advisors. Following their defeat, the UIC threatened to engage in Guerrilla warfare to regain control of the country. Many UIC militiamen had been driven into hiding but launched attacks against the Ethiopian and TFG forces which endures to this day.

At this point, the Somali people's fate, for an indefinite time period, was sealed when a militant, splinter group of the UIC decided to continue the battle against the TFG until their defeat. Al Shabaab emerged after the UIC splintered into small factions in 2006. Al Shabaab threatened by covenant to wage a jihad against the enemies of Islam and is to this day engaged in combat against the TFG.

Somali Islamists and opposition leaders met in Asmara, capital of Eritrea, to unite in order to fight the TFG and the occupation of Somalia by Ethiopian forces. Approximately 400 delegates attended the meeting and formed a new organization called the Alliance for the Re-liberation of Somalia (ARS). By May 2008, the organization was divided over whether to join the peace talks with the new official government of Somalia.

After the defeat of the UIC, representatives of the TFG and ARS participated in a peace conference in Djibouti on May 31, 2008. The Djibouti Agreement, signed on August 18, succeeded in bringing together opposing political groups which led to the formation of a new government and its subsequent transfer to Mogadishu in early 2009. Terms of the Agreement included the departure from Somalia of Ethiopian forces by 2009 and the continued presence of AMISOM.

Not all opposition groups supported the Agreement or new government since radical Islamists, other clans and militia forces continued to oppose the TFG. In addition, the conditions in Somalia during the decades of conflict, lack of development, poverty, despair and hopelessness spawned criminal elements who engaged in criminal activities such as piracy and taking control of seaports and airstrips.

As of January 2009, Ethiopian troops withdrew from Somalia following a two year insurgency leaving the TFG in power. On the other hand, Ethiopia had lost territory and power to Al Shabaab. The government in Somalia was now occupied by a power-sharing group consisting of an Islamic splinter group led by Sheikh Sharif Ahmed's

Alliance for the Re-liberation of Somalia (ARS) and the TFG led by Prime Minister Nur Hassan. ARS leader Sheikh Ahmed was elected president on January 31, 2009.

The TFG was not seeking to establish peace and stability as had been the case with the UIC but seemed more interested in perpetuating themselves in power. They were guilty of violating the human rights of the people of Somalia as recorded by Human Rights watch:

> Many abuses investigated by Human Rights Watch – including most of those described below – are not isolated incidents involving a few armed men claiming to be TFG security personnel. Frequently, abuses occurred in the context of large-scale TFG security operations, such as house-to-house search and seizure operations across whole neighborhoods of Mogadishu. (Muhammad Megalommatis, *The Destruction of Mogadishu: Genocidal Plans and Practises...*, Afro articles, June 29, 2008)

Shortly thereafter, on February 8, 2009, fighting erupted in Mogadishu as the battle for control of the capital was renewed as was the battle for the province of Bakool, the city of Hudur and Baidoa. During these battles, hundreds of militiamen and civilians died.

By May 11, 2009, after fierce fighting in Mogadishu, the rebels gained the upper hand although the fighting continued until May 14 without the rebels gaining complete control of the capital while tens of thousands of civilians were displaced.

Facing defeat of his government, Sheikh Adam Mohamed Nuur Madobe, the Transitional Government speaker, pleaded for assistance from the international community. On July 17, 2009, after two French security advisors were kidnaped, French warships and helicopters were sent to Somalia to free the hostages while at the same time, the U.S. launched helicopter attacks against the rebels.

From 2009 to 2011, fierce battles were waged between the TFG and the rebels with the rebels maintaining the upper hand. On February 20, 2011, AMISON troops entered the fray and began to score a number of victories over the rebels. By March 5, AMISON and TFG forces claimed control over six of the cities districts, six were contested and three were controlled by the rebels.

On August 11, 2011, TFG and AMISON forces managed to gain control over the entire capital although the rebels continued with hit and run attacks.

One of U.S. objectives in Somalia was to destroy any opportunity for an Islamic government to gain control over the country again. Since the rebels were persevering with their insurgency against the TFG and their allies, the United States decided to take further action to stamp out any vestiges of a real Islamic force.

This time, Washington's proxy was the armed forces of Kenya who alleged without giving any evidence or proof that Al Shabaab was crossing the border from Somalia into Kenya and kidnapping people at random. Kenya then claimed that the kidnappings were destroying their tourist industry and that they had no choice but to deploy soldiers in Somalia to fight the so-called terrorists and drive them a long way from the border.

No sooner had the operation commenced when the West suddenly threw its support behind Kenya. While the actual fighting was carried out by the Kenya forces, the TFG and Ethiopian forces, additional support was coming from the U.S., Denmark, Israel and France.

In an effort to end the acts of terrorism perpetrated by al Shabaab in Kenya, 2,400 Kenyan troops crossed the border into southern Somalia on October 16, 2011. To enhance its war against terrorism in Somalia, Washington has provided military support to Kenya and according to the Center for International and Strategic Studies, "Some sources suggest that the Kenyans have received as much as another $3 billion in security and military support from the United States since September 11, 2001." (31) Congressional Research Service reveals that, "Kenya is a major African recipient of Department of Defense training and equipment." (32) Kenyan troops fought alongside TFG and AMISOM forces.

In actual fact, the Kenya government had been coordinating the attacks with the Pentagon. According to Scott Gration, U.S. Ambassador to Kenya, "We are looking to see how, as an ally in this conflict on terrorism, we can help the Kenyans." (Andre Vltchek, *Grab Everything and Justify it by War*, Counterpunch, April 6-8 2012)

As well, Jean-Philippe Rémy of the Guardian Weekly reported that:

> Several sources agree, however, that the Kenyan intervention plan was discussed and decided in 2010, then finalized with input from western partners, including the U.S. and to a lesser extent France. Nairobi seems to have seized on kidnappings of foreign nationals by Somali groups on Kenya territory as an excuse to launch an operation ready and waiting. (ibid)

The leader of the Social Democratic party of Kenya, Mwandawiro Mghanga, reported that, "So things are done behind closed doors and people know very well that the Kenya National Intelligence and the army cooperate very closely with the U.S. (ibid)

Uganda and Burundi, who supplied troops to AMISON, occupied the vacuum created by the withdrawal of Ethiopian troops and served as the United States main proxies in Somalia in the battle to hunt down and kill members of al Shabaab. Fierce fighting between the AMISOM and al Shabaab left behind a trail of humanitarian catastrophes. According to Human Rights Watch, "All told, some 63,000 people were driven from their homes…across southern and central Somalia during the first three weeks of the year." (30)

By 2010, al Shabaab had control of more territory than the TFG, notwithstanding the presence of thousands of U.S.-backed AMISOM troops, but two developments foreshadowed the end of al Shabaab's ascendancy in Somalia and the reappearance of the semblance of a stable society. One was the Kenyan incursion into Somalia to destroy al Shabaab and the other the emergence of an Islamic group known as ASWJ who opposed the influence of al Shabaab.

Ahlu Sunna Waljama'a or ASWJ, a Somalian paramilitary organization, founded in the 1990s as a quasi-political organization dedicated to Sufi religious scholarship, emerged as one of the more powerful organizations dedicated to destroying al Shabaab. Ethiopia empowered ASWJ by arming, financing and training their fighters to enable them to conduct a series of major offences against al Shabaab. In addition to its military contribution to the war against al Shabaab, they struck a power sharing agreement with the TFG

Furthermore, French ships and American drones targeted al Shabaab strongholds referred to in a Global Research article stating that, "A combined force of U.S. predator drones and French naval vessels is targeting four towns in the Southern region so that Kenyan military forces on the ground can seize Kismayo, a port city under the control of al-Shabaab. The city is a major source of trade and serves as a lifeline for the resistance movement." (33)

By 2012, AMISOM, U.S. and French military support, ASWJ and Ethiopian and Kenyan forces have transformed the profile of Southern Somalia driving al Shabaab from all the major towns although their acts of terrorism did not end. A cycle of violence between al Shabaab and Kenya culminated on September 21, 2013 with an al Shabaab attack on the Westgate Mall in Nairobi in which 72 people were killed.

Somalia has finally reached a crossroads in its journey towards stability, security and an opportunity for development by the fall of 2012. A new federal government or SFG has "won the support and recognition of the international community." (34)

Nevertheless, the SFG remains vulnerable and dependent on African troops to protect its leaders and defend its sovereignty. (35)

Foreign intervention, particularly by the United States has undermined the potential for the people of Somalis to resolve their internal struggles without foreign influences seeking their own ends. Support for Barre and destroying the UIC were both detrimental to the development, security and safety of Somalia. In fact, the United States created the very problem it was dedicated to eradicating.

Resorting to illegal methods of warfare is standard practice for the United States and drone attacks are in that category. Since World War II, the U.S. has used the atomic bombs, Napalm, Agent Orange, Cluster Bombs, depleted uranium weapons, white phosphorous and Drones, all of which are banned by international law including the Geneva Conventions and the UN Convention on Certain Conventional Weapons.

Drones have been used against "suspected" Islamic rebels in Somalia. Bear in mind that frequently the targets are merely suspects with no assurance that they or the people nearby are actually terrorists. Firing drones into a country that you are not at war with is illegal according to the UN Charter, Chapters Six and Seven. Assassination is prohibited both by U.S. domestic law and international law violating the principle of the rule of law which guarantees each suspect due process and honoring their civil and legal rights. Many innocent civilians have been killed by drones which violates the Geneva Conventions.

A legal argument can be adduced to proof that the use of drones is illegal in both international and domestic law. Washington's argument for the legality of assassination through the use of drones is based on the *Authorization for Use of United States Armed Forces* which states that:

> The President is authorized to use all necessary and appropriate force against those nations, organizations, or persons he determines planned, authorized, committed or aided terrorist attacks that occurred on September 11, 2001, or harbored such organizations or persons, in order to prevent any future acts against the United States by such nations, organizations or persons.

This authorization is limited to persons who were part of the terrorist act of 9/11. To justify drone assassinations, the president would have to prove that such persons who are targeted were not only part of 9/11 but pose a threat currently to the security of the United States.

Then there is the problem posed by the United Nations Charter which prohibits such aggressive acts other than an act of self-defence against an imminent threat. Article 51 of the UN Charter states that:

> Nothing in the present Charter shall impair the inherent right of individual or collective self-defense if an armed attack occurs against a Member of the United Nations, until the Security Council has taken measures necessary to maintain international peace and security.

Note that Article 51 clearly states that an "armed attack" is already underway; nevertheless an imminent threat is considered to offer similar justification. The standard interpretation of imminent threat is based on the Caroline test which states that:

> Anticipatory self-defence...holds that it may be justified only in cases in which "necessity of that self-defence" is instant, overwhelming and leaving no choice of means, and no moment for deliberation.

The use of drones to assassinate terrorists does not come close to meeting the Caroline test.

The imperative of Article 51 in the UN Charter applies in every case when drones are used by the United States due to the fact that the Charter became part of U.S. law upon ratification of the Charter in 1945. According to the United Nations:

> It is a basic principle of international law that a State party to an international treaty must ensure that its own domestic law are consistent with what is required by the treaty.

American law is secondary to treaties signed by the United States according to Article 6 of the American Constitution which states that, "All treaties made, or which shall be made, under the Authority of the United States, shall be the supreme Law of the Land."

Assassinating suspected terrorists with drones clearly violates the UN Charter and the Articles of the Charter have become the supreme law of the land overriding the Authorization for the Use of Force. It is irrefutable that the use of drones for the purpose of assassination is illegal.

Statistics for U.S. drone strikes in Somalia from 2007 to 2013:

Total U.S. drone strikes: 3-9

Total reported killed: 58 – 170

Civilians reported killed: 11-57

Children reported killed: 1-3

(The Bureau of Investigative Journalism, *Covert drone War*, January 2013)

As of October 2012, 1.3 million people were internally displaced and over one million fled to other countries. Approximately 10.7

million people are in dire need of humanitarian assistance due to malnutrition, homelessness and disease. The United Nations Refugee Agency (UNHCR) has agreed to provide 30% of the daily food requirement to a million Somali refugees rather than allow them to die from malnutrition. Somalia now has one of the highest malnutrition rates in the world.

Western countries are not addressing the problems in Somalia because it does not serve their interests. Although the U.S. has claimed to have engaged in a number of humanitarian interventions including Serbia, Libya, Iraq and Afghanistan, these actions were not humanitarian interventions but were war crimes, but when a real humanitarian disaster screams for assistance, it fall on deaf ears.

Devastation barely begins to describe the impact of the machinations of American intervention in Somalia which included supporting corrupt and brutal dictators or governments, overthrowing a government whom they wrongly claimed were terrorists and persuading and supporting two client states to intervene in Somalia. Although a number of other factors contributed to the tragedy in Somalia, America's role was critical.

Somalia was nothing more than a colony to the U.S. and to the other powers which had intervened and they exploited Somalia for their own national interests. The catchphrase "national interests" is frequently misused by government officials and academics by interpreting the meaning to include the whole population when, in fact, only the elites really gain from their government's foreign pursuits. In other words, the U.S. is stealing from the poor to give to the rich.

CHAPTER 3

Libya

The motive for the U.S. participation in the Libyan "humanitarian" campaign pertains to the refusal of Gadhafi to support American plans for the region and his attempts to create an independent Africa free of American influence. He had challenged the institutions of global capital such as the World Bank, IMF and WTO and persuaded other African countries not to participate in American military alliances, in particular, AFRICOM. In addition, Gadhafi was determined to build a more unified Africa in terms of trade and security creating a continent more independent of Western powers.

Gadhafi was also assuming a leadership role in Africa for the purpose of preventing the continent from becoming a supplier of cheap labor and raw materials for Western countries and, in particular, for the United States. As well, he was undermining opportunities for U.S. investment and economic exploitation. For example, he was frustrating attempts by Bechtel and caterpillar to gain a foothold in Libya and was instead turning to Russia, China and Germany.

Libyan plans for an African central bank to issue a single African currency would have threatened the ability of Western powers to exploit the continent. Once Africa had established its own currency, Western powers would have to conduct trade in gold rather than in their own currencies which can be expanded by their own central banks. As well, An African monetary fund would critically weaken Western countries ability to impose economic conditions attached to the money lent to African countries by the IMF. The IMF imposed these conditionalities to eliminate any trade barriers employed by the developing country, to open the countries' markets to western corporations, to offer investment opportunities through devalued currency or privatization and to introduce neoliberal policies. In other words, the IMF created an enormous opportunity for exploitation of developing countries by Western countries.

Gadhafi was formulating plans for a common security system for all of Africa. In a 2004 African Union Summit in Sirte, Libya, African nations agreed on a Common African Defense and Security Charter stipulating that "any attack against an African country is considered an attack against the Continent as a whole." To execute the common defence agreement, an African Standby Force was created in 2010 with a mandate to uphold and implement the Charter.

Successive American administrations since President Carter have coveted the potential for oil and the unrestricted access to strategic ports in the Indian Ocean and Red Sea. As is usually the case, Washington's real motivation had to be hidden behind a veil of lofty but specious justifications which the public would readily accept. In the case of Libya, the U.S. concocted a story about the urgent need for humanitarian intervention to put an end to Gadhafi's atrocities against his own people.

In fact, the specious justification is easily exposed by NATO's illegal blockage of ceasefire negotiations that had been called for in the UN resolution and organized by the AU. The AU team had been prevented from flying to Libya. Significantly, Gadhafi's agreement with the AU plan renders any international attempt to intervene totally superfluous. According to Thabo Mbeki, past president of South Africa:

> On March 10, 2011, the AU Peace and Security Council adopted a roadmap for the peaceful resolution of the then Libya conflict. Among other things, this roadmap provided for an end to the violent conflict in Libya. The African Union secured the agreement of the Gaddafi regime to this Roadmap, replying on the fact that Libya is one of its members. The AU forwarded its March 10 decision to the United Nations, the League of Arab States and other relevant organizations. On March 17, seven days after the African Union had its Roadmap for the peaceful resolution of the Libyan conflict, it adopted its Resolution 1973 which created the space for NATO...to intervene in Libya to impose a violent resolution of this conflict, centred on regime change, which objective was completely at variance with Resolution 1973. (Thabo Mbeki, *Reflections on Peacemaking, State Sovereignty and democratic Governance in Africa*, University of the Western Cape, Community Law Centre, February 16,2012)

Proof that the United States' real objective was regime change is the fact that the CIA was grooming various people to assume leadership roles in a post-Gadhafi era in addition to training military staff to be part of an insurgency (see below).

Notwithstanding the frequent reports by the media of Gadhafi atrocities, evidence for these tragedies has not been evinced. According to Patrick Cockburn in the International:

> Ever since the Libyan uprising started on 15 February, the foreign media have regurgitated stories of atrocities carried out by Gaddafi's forces. It is now becoming clear that reputable human rights organisations such as Amnesty International and Human Rights Watch have been unable to find evidence for the worst of these.
> (Patrick Cockburn, *Don't believe everything you read about Gaddafi*, June 26, 2011)

Although UN Resolution 1973 provided the U.S. and NATO with a mandate to protect civilians in Libya, it became a cover for their actual intentions to create an opportunity to pursue their real objective of overthrowing Gadhafi.

Refuting the pretext of a humanitarian intervention, Barak Obama, David Cameron and Nicolas Sarkozy wrote an op-ed piece in the New York Times on April 15, 2011, in which they stated: "But it is impossible to imagine a future for Libya with Qaddafi in power…any deal that leaves him in power would lead to further chaos…so long as Qaddafi is in power, NATO must maintain its operations."

Violations of UN Resolution 1973 include the weapons supplied to the rebels, NATO weapons used against Gadhafi forces and the supply of military personnel on the ground assisting rebel forces. In addition, NATO forces provided air cover for the rebel forces bombing towns or any obstacles on their march to the capital. Libyan rebels who triumphed in their six-month uprising against Colonel Muammar Qaddafi could not have prevailed without arms, air cover, funding and diplomatic support from NATO and Arab allies.

As well, NATO warplanes bombed the pipe factory in Brega killing six people. These pipes were used to repair the man-made irrigation system that supplies water to 70% of the Libyan people and is critical to repairing and maintaining their water supply.

The town of Sirte was targeted by NATO forces due to its importance as a centre for creating an independent Africa during the period when the African Union was founded there in 1999 and was proposed as the capital for a United States of Africa. It was a symbolic target for NATO who wanted to send a message to all of Africa that it should prepare for a new round of exploitation. (Daniel Kovalik, *Libya and Creative Destruction*, November 21, 2012)

Rockets and mortars levelled Sirte to the ground leaving it without a single building intact or any infrastructure. Military actions in Sirte were clearly unrelated to any humanitarian campaign to protect civilians.

Furthermore, it is clear from Amnesty International reports that innocent people were targeted without any reasonable justification as reported in an AI study in March 2012 which disclosed that:

> Dozens of civilians have been killed in NATO airstrikes on private homes in residential and rural areas where Amnesty International, UN experts, other international NGOs and journalists found no evidence of military objectives at the strike locations at the time of the strikes. (Amnesty International, The Forgotten Victims of NATO Airstrikes, March 2012, p.7)

Reinforcing the suspicion that the U.S. and NATO leaders were embarked on a mission to establish a more Western-friendly leader in Libya was the speedy recognition of the National Transitional

Council (NTC) and its appointment of the first post-Gadhafi Prime Minister, Abdurrahim El Keib.

The Western-approved government, the NTC, drafted election laws that would exclude a majority of Libyans from running for office. According to the Wall Street Journal (January 3, 2012), the new election law: "appears most ambitious…in laying out more than 20 classes of people who will be prohibited to stand as candidates in the vote" and "Could be used to against three-quarters of the country."

In addition to the new electoral laws, the new prime minister, El Keib: "has sent Libya on a bumpy road towards democracy by naming a cabinet of secularists and thereby snubbing prominent Islamists" according to the Guardian (November 2011). The Guardian claims that: "The cabinet is likely to find approval from Libya's Western backers, concerned about hardline Islamists. Such a move might be welcomed by its Western supporters but will trigger strong opposition from the Islamists especially since they were an important part of the revolution against Gaddafi."

The most revealing manifestation of the NATO agenda to establish a Western-oil-friendly government in Libya is the background of the people who have assumed leadership roles in the post-Gadhafi Libya.

The President El Keib, who had been in the United States since 1975, was chosen by the NTC on October 31, 2011. He was a professor of Electrical Engineering at the University of Alabama where his research was sponsored by such entities as the Electric Power Research Institute, the United States Department of Energy and the Alabama Power Company. In 2006, he resigned his position at the University of Alabama to become Chair of the Petroleum Institute in the UAE which is funded by several international oil companies such as Royal Dutch Shell, BP, Total and the Japan Oil Development Company as well as having connections to the University of Maryland, University of Texas at Austin and Rice University. In the summer of 2011, he quit his position at the Institute to join the NTC after a 36 year absence from Libya.

Another key figure in the rebellion was Mahmoud Jibril who served as the interim Prime Minister as a member of the NTC for a period of seven and one half months during the civil war. He did his graduate studies in the U.S. at the University of Pittsburgh finishing in 1985, followed by a number of years of teaching at the same university under Richard Cottam, a former U.S. intelligence officer. From 2007 to 2011, he served in the Gaddafi Regime as Head of the National Economic Development Board. According to the Boston Globe (March 28, 2011), Jibril: "played a key role in persuading the United States and its allies" to militarily intervene against Gaddafi.

In a leaked U.S. diplomatic cable written on November 2009, Gene Cretz, America's ambassador to Libya, described Jibril as: "as serious interlocutor who 'gets' the US perspective." In the cable, Jibril also regrets that: "The US spoiled a golden opportunity to capitalize on its 'soft power' after the fall of the Soviet Union in 1989 by putting 'boots on the ground' in the Middle East."

Another pro-American ex-pat, Kalifa Haftar, was appointed leader of Libya's opposition military forces by the NTC. As another Libyan ex-pat living in the United States since the early 1990s until his return after the February 127th uprising, Haftar lived in suburban Virginia only a few miles from Langley suspiciously unemployed for the entire period of his stay.

On May 17, 1991 the Washington Times reported that: "three hundred and fifty Libyans would arrive soon in the United States. . . . [and] . . . were trained by our CIA to topple President Gadhafi." (Enver Masud, *Who's Terrorizing Whom*, Washington Times, May 17, 1991) In another article published in the Real News, it was reported that:

> Many members of the Ansar al-Shariah militia are veterans of the CIA sponsored Afghanistan war against the Soviet Union. Ansar al-Shariah is now a powerful militia group in Benghazi. They were one of the fighting forces that received CIA support in overthrowing Muammar Gadhafi in 2011. (David William Pear, "Benghazi-gate": A Window into the Secret War in Libya by the CIA, The Real News, November 15, 2012)

The Immigration and Refugee Board of Canada quoted from the book *Manipulations Africaines* indicating that: "Haftar, created and financed by the CIA in Chad, vanished into thin air with the help of the CIA." (Immigration and Refugee Board of Canada, *Libya: The Djava Khalifa Haftar movement*, May 2006) As well, the Jamestown Foundation, based in Washington, D.C., published a study in which it reported that: "Not only did the CIA sponsor and fund the LNA (Libyan National Army), it engineered the entry of the LNA officers and men into the United States where they established a training camp." (Dario Cristiani, Michael W. S. Ryan, Camille Tawil and Jacob Zenn; *Elections Issue: Militants in Libyan Politics*, Jamestown Foundation, Volume 1 Issue 3, August 16, 2012)

Hence three of the high ranking members of the Libyan opposition spent an extended period of time in the United States and two of them conveniently appeared just when they were needed in the civil war. All of them have close ties to various institutions in the U.S. According to Thabo Mbeki:

> Having become slaves to the regime-change objective, the relevant United Nations institutions betrayed all the prescriptions they are obliged by international law to respect... Thus: the UN Security Council surrendered its authority to oversee the future of Libya to a self-appointed 'Libya Contact Group' made up of countries and organizations committed to regime-change in Libya, in defiance of the security Council decisions...They [Security Council and office of the Secretary-General] chose to give free reign to the so-called P3, the United States, France and the United Kingdom of Great Britain and North Ireland, exclusively to decide the future of Libya.

(Thabo Mbeki, *Reflections on Peacemaking, State Sovereignty and democratic Governance in Africa*, University of the Western Cape, Community Law Centre, February 16,2012)

Most revealing of all is the blueprint that NATO has drawn up for post-Gadhafi Libya. Prior to the war, Libya had no debts and was a creditor nation until NATO countries froze $150 billion in Libyan assets. Ironically, after inflicting extensive damage on the Libyan infrastructure and freezing assets, the World Bank has offered to loan money to the NTC for reconstruction and development. According to a World Bank press release:

The Bank has been asked to examine the need for repair and restoration of services in the water, energy and transport sectors and in cooperation with the International Monetary Fund, to support budget preparation and help the banking sector on its feet

(World Bank, *World Bank to Help Libya to Rebuild and Deliver Essential Services to Citizens*, September 13, 2011).

Furthermore, even before Gadhafi had been brutally murdered, U.S. Ambassador Gene Cretz was on the phone with 150 American companies discussing business opportunities in Libya. As well, according to an article in *Ventures*, "General Electric…expects to generate as much as $10b in revenue in Libya, as the North African country aims to rebuild its economy, infrastructure, and institutions in the post-Gadhafi era." (Ventures Africa, *Rebuilding Libya: GE Eyes up to $10 bn in Revenue*, May 31, 2012)

Rebels supported by the United States and the NTC have been guilty of human rights atrocities in the post-Gadhafi regime. Reprisals, vindictiveness and racism have motivated the NATO-supported rebels to murder their perceived enemies. According to Wuill Morrow from Global Research:

> The Libyan Transnational Council (TNC) regime installed by the US-NATO intervention in Libya last year is responsible for ongoing atrocities, particularly against black-skinned Libyans, detainees and other alleged supporters of the previous Gaddafi government…Amnesty International and Doctors Without Borders have recently published statements protesting against the systematic abuse and torture of prisoners in detention centres controlled by the TNC and tribes.

(Will Morrow, *Ongoing atrocities by NATO-installed regime*,
Global Research, February 12, 2012)

Atrocities and war crimes committed by the new regime and the
rebel forces under its control exposes the lie that the U.S. and
NATO were performing a humanitarian mission. The people who
were protected against Gadhafi's humanitarian atrocities are now
themselves perpetrating human rights atrocities. Although Gadhafi
wasn't actually guilty of a humanitarian crisis, U.S. and NATO are
guilty of two human rights atrocities: the bombing and unleashing of
a rebel group who committed atrocities. Will Morrow condemns "The
Transitional Libyan National Council (TNC) regime installed by the
US-NATO intervention in Libya last year is responsible for ongoing
atrocities." (ibid)

Gadhafi supporters were subjected to terrible reprisals which were
both tragic and alarming. Many of Gadhafi's supporters have been
arrested, beaten tortured and killed. In an Amnesty International
Report, it was revealed that:

> Opposition fighters and supporters have abducted, arbitrarily detained, tortured
> and killed former members of the security forces, suspected al-Gaddafi loyalists,
> captured soldiers and foreign nationals wrongly suspected of being mercenaries
> fighting on behalf of al-Gaddafi forces. (Amnesty international, *The
> Battle for Libya: Killings, Disappearances and Torture*, May,
> 2011)

Black people in Libya were also the victims of atrocities perpetrated
by the rebels. An Amnesty International report states that: "From the
start of the Libyan rebellion black people in Libya have been attacked

and lynched by rebel mobs." (Amnesty International, *Amnesty and racist rebel atrocities in Libya*, August 31, 2011)

In addition to the atrocities against particular groups in Libya, a number of cities were heavily bombed rendering them virtually unliveable. NATO bombing had almost levelled Sirte to the ground, pulverized by rocket or mortar fire, and destroyed its infrastructure. On September 15, 2011, NATO jets and drones specifically and knowingly targeted civilians including 47 civilian rescuers. Deliberately bombing a second time to kill rescue workers is known as double tapping and is a heinous crime which violates the Geneva Conventions. (Maximillan C. Forte, *Slouching Towards Sirte: NATO's War on Libya and Africa*, January 4, 2013)

Other cities were subject to the same treatment as reported by Amnesty International, "Given the atrocities committed in Misrata and Benghazi the option of allowing the rebels to conquer pro-Gaddafi population centres is inconceivable." (Amnesty International, *Amnesty and racist rebel atrocities in Libya*, August 31, 2011)

In total, U.S.-led NATO forces flew 10,000 bombing sorties over Libya dropping 40,000 bombs over a period of eight months. The destructive capability of NATO's bombing campaign clearly demonstrates that their objective was not humanitarian in nature but was designed to provide air cover to the rebels. Their heavy bombing was a blatant violation of UN Resolution 1973.

After the "humanitarian" mission ended, The NTC formed a temporary government until elections could be held with Jalil as the chairman of the informal executive team and the council serving as the legislative body on March 5, 2012. On July 7 2012, the General National Council won the first election and took office on August 8.

Just as Yugoslavia had been held together by Tito and degenerated into a war in each of the federations with different groups in each federation fighting for control of a new independent state, the same fate befell Libya. Cities and militias did not consider themselves to be under the authority of the government in Tripoli and operated independently of the central government. In the economic sphere, investors and the IMF viewed Libya as an opportunity for exploitation.

Esam Mohamed writing for the Associated Press summarizes the problems in post-Gadhafi Libya as:

> The transitional government failed to unite powerful militias under a national army. Instead, the militias and rival tribes often clash from their power bases in different parts of the country. Also, eastern Libya complains it is under-represented in the new government, as it was under Gadhafi, and there is talk of setting up a semi-autonomous government there. (Esam Mohamed, *Libya's transitional rulers hand over power, Associated Press*, August 8, 2012)

As well, "the Transitional National Council [TNC], have failed to secure important military facilities in the south" which fell under the control of local tribal groups "who are also well known for their traditional smuggling pursuits." (Andrew McGregor, *Tribes and Terrorism: The Emerging Security Threat from Libya's lawless South*, Jamestown Foundation, January 25, 2013)

Militias are unwilling to support the central government and seem to enjoy impunity for their many crimes including arbitrary detention, torture and murder. An Amnesty International report reveals that:

> Armed militias operating across Libya commit widespread human rights abuses with impunity, fueling insecurity and hindering the rebuilding of state institutions. The report…documents widespread and serious abuses, including war crimes, by a multitude of militias against suspected al-Gaddafi loyalists with cases of people being unlawfully detained and tortured – sometimes to death.

(Amnesty International, *Libya: 'Out of control' militias commit widespread abuses, a year on from the uprising*, February 15, 2012)

Tribesmen are separating themselves from the NTC and in some instances declaring their independence. In March, a meeting of 3,000 tribesman and leaders in Eastern Libya, proclaimed an autonomous state with Benghazi as its capital.

In the South, a militia based on the Toubou ethnic group clashed with Arab tribesman and reactivated the separatist movement Toubou Front for the Salvation of Libya.

In the north, fighting broke out when long-standing rivalries erupted in Zuwara with Berber militiamen battling pro-Gadhafi Arabs from Jamail and Raghdalin.

Another critical problem prevailing in post-Gadhafi Libya is the looting of weapons caches with the weapons flowing to Mali and

Niger. Even worse, some of the weapons are reaching the hands of al Qaeda groups. The Huffington posts warn that:

> As a result [outflow of weapons], senior military officers say that they are bracing for a long, persistent new campaign against the Islamic militias clustered around the al Qaeda offshoot called the Islamic Maghreb (AQIM), which has absorbed most of the weapons spreading across Mali, Niger and northern Nigeria. U.S. officials say they believe AQIM is actively engaged in equipping and training jihadist militias across North Africa. (Huffington Post, *Libyan Weapons Arming Al Qaeda Militias Across North Africa*, February 21, 2013)

Before U.S.-led NATO "humanitarian intervention", Libya was ruled by a brutal dictator but also a benevolent dictator in the sense that he spent the revenues from oil on health, education and other social programs elevating the country to number one in Africa on the UN Development index. After the "humanitarian intervention", Libya has been fraught with out-of-control militias seeking independence or clashing with other militias, an outflow of weapons to al Qaeda groups, no widely respected central government and a country in which few investors would be willing to risk their money. President Obama cannot honestly boast "mission accomplished".

CHAPTER 4

Ethiopia

Ethiopia has become an anti-terrorist outpost for the United States by providing bases for drones and secret prisons for terrorist suspects who are denied due process or respect for their rights. When Ethiopia invaded Somalia to overthrow a moderate Islamic government, it served as a proxy for the United States in its war against terrorism. In return for serving its master, Ethiopia is a major recipient of U.S. economic and military aid.

United States officials develop a sudden case of impaired vision when they prop up a government despite its horrendous record on human rights. Domestic law, international law and moral issues take a back seat to American economic and strategic interest. Pragmatic idealism, a major foreign policy doctrine, developed by U.S. academics, foreign policy wonks and intellectuals, describes a foreign policy that masquerades as honoring the ideals of human rights, compassion and conforming to the law but, in fact, is designed to serve American corporate and elite interests.

For example, the 1995 election in which Meles Zenawi and his party, the Ethiopian People's Revolutionary Democratic Front (EPRDF), won 86% of the seats was widely criticized as illegitimate. Human Rights watch reports that:

> Led by the Ethiopian People's Revolutionary Democratic Front (EPRDF), the government has used donor-sponsored programs, salaries, and training opportunities as political weapons to control the population, punish dissent, and undermine political opponents-both real and perceived. Local officials deny these people access to seeds and fertilizer, agricultural land, credit, food aid, and other resources for development...Ethiopia's foreign donors are well aware of this discrimination, but have little to address the problem or tackling their own problem in underwriting government repression. (Human Rights Watch, *Development Without Freedom: How Aid Underwrites Repression in Ethiopia*, October 2010)

The New York Times also reported on the illegitimacy of the elections by pointing out that;

> Mr. Meles was undoubtedly a strongman. Despite being one of the United States' closest allies on the continent, Mr. Meles repeatedly jailed dissidents and journalists, intimidated opponents and their supporters to win mind-boggling one-sided elections, and oversaw brutal campaigns in restive areas of the country where Ethiopian military has raped and killed many civilians.
> (Jeffrey Gettleman, *Ethiopian Leader's Death Highlights Gap Between U.S. Interests and Ideals*, New York Times, April 21, 2012)

Subsequent elections until his death in 2012 were equally replete with the same human rights atrocities yet Zenawi continued to enjoy support from the United States government. Human

Rights Watch wrote a letter to President Obama concerning his government's support for a brutal and corrupt dictator in which it stated that:

> After more than two decades of Meles Zenawi's leadership, Ethiopia's institutions have become mere extensions of the ruling party power. The country has grown steadily more authoritarian since the 2005 elections ended in bloodshed and controversy. The ruling party won more than 99 per cent of the seats in both 2008 local government elections and the 2010 parliamentary elections, mainly due to the government's comprehensive crackdown on dissent. (Human Rights Watch, *Development Without Freedom: How Aid Underwrites Repression in Ethiopia*, October 10)

For example, United States officials knew that the elections in 2005 were fraudulent since they and the EU served as observers and reported that they "fell short of international standards."

One of the reasons that the U.S. was willing to overlook the illegitimate elections and human rights atrocities in Ethiopia was due to its role of a surrogate army for the United States or according to journalist Thomas C. Mountain "muscle for what passes for foreign policy in East Africa." (Thomas C. Mountain, *The Ethiopia Files*, Counterpunch, September 7, 2011) Ethiopia invaded Somalis and Eritrea for the United States.

One of the major atrocities bordering on genocide that is overlooked by the United States has been the Ethiopian crusade to eradicate all the Somalis living in the Ogaden region of Ethiopia who were struggling to become part of Somalia.

To understand the problem, the history of decolonization needs to be examined. The Italian military had invaded Abyssinia in 1936 but were ousted by the allied forces in 1941 when Britain established military rule over the territory. There has been a long history of disputes over land in the former Abyssinia culminating in a decision by the British to restore Ethiopian sovereignty over the Ogaden region in 1948. Ogaden was a territory populated to a large extent by the Somali people. Opinion was split in the Ogaden region over union with Somalia with some Somalis preferring to remain part of Ethiopia while Somali nationalists objected.

When Somalia gained independence in 1960, it embarked on a campaign to unite all Somali territories including Ogaden. Over the next decades, the Somalia government supported insurgencies inside Ethiopia and embarked on military incursions across the border. In 1976, with the overthrow of Haile Selassie, Somalia's President Sid Barre began supporting rebel groups in Ogaden ultimately leading to the formation of the Ogaden National Liberation Front (ONLF). ONLF's aggressive efforts to establish self-determination in the Ogaden Region was met with strong measures by the Ethiopian government to maintain tight security in the Somali Regional State over the people and the local government.

Inevitably, both sides resorted to armed warfare with ONLF guerrillas pitted against the Ethiopian army. Pursuant to an American-backed Ethiopian invasion of Somalia in 2006, warfare between the ONLF and Ethiopian forces escalated to the point where Prime Minister Zenawi announced on June 9, 2007, that he was mounting a major counter-insurgency campaign to suppress the ONLF rebellion.

The counterinsurgency dramatically escalated when the ONLF attacked a Chinese oil installation in the Somali Region in April 2007, killing more than 70 Chinese. In justifying their actions, the rebels accused the oil companies of destroying the livelihood of the local population, causing massive starvation, and preventing them from growing crops by clearing their land.

In addition, Zenawi's counterinsurgency strategy was not only to destroy the insurgents but to destroy their base of support, the nationalist Somalis living in Ogaden. To accomplish these objectives, Zenawi cut off economic resources to the region, forced massive relocations, destroyed villages, killed civilians on a large scale, and engaged in torture and rape. Over 170,000 Ogaden refugees fled to Daadaab, a massive camp in Kenya.

Human Rights Watch has documented the atrocities in a major study which reports that:

> Tens of thousands of ethnic Somali civilians living in eastern Ethiopia's Somali Regional State are experiencing serious abuses and a looming humanitarian crisis in the context of a little-known conflict between the Ethiopian government and an Ethiopian Somali rebel movement. The situation is critical. Since the mid-2007 thousands of people have fled, seeking refuge in neighboring Somalia and Kenya from widespread Ethiopian military attacks on civilians and villages that amount to war crimes and crimes against humanity. (Human Rights Watch, *Collective Punishment: War Crimes in the Ogaden area of Ethiopia*, June, 2008)

The ubiquitous and brutal character of the atrocities is also described in the same Human Watch report as:

> The widespread and apparently systematic nature of the attacks on villages throughout Somali Region is strong evidence that the killings, torture, rape and forced displacement are also crimes against humanity for which the Ethiopian government bears ultimate responsibility. (ibid)

As in any guerrilla war, support of the population is critical to the success of the rebellion. As a counterinsurgency measure to undermine popular support, the Ethiopian government had ordered civilians to relocate from small villages to designated towns, giving them two to seven days to move. To ensure that the people comply with the order to evacuate their towns and settlements, the government implemented a graduated system of terror from confiscation and killing livestock to public executions and burning villages. Human Rights Watch has reported that 87 villages had been burned and "forcefully evacuated during government military operations." (ibid)

Many of the refugees have fled to neighboring countries such as Somalia and Kenya while others languished in internally displaced camps (IDC).

Rape has been widespread and very common in the Ogaden region where women and girls have been sexually assaulted repeatedly by soldiers and officers.

Arbitrary arrest, detention, abuse, torture and execution involving persons of all ages have been reported by Human Rights Watch. All these human rights abuses are violations of international law and are considered war crimes.

Compounding the human rights catastrophe was the drought and inability of 75 million people to feed themselves and their families, reflecting the fact that 90% of the population lives on less than one dollar a day despite the infusion of two billion dollars a day from the UK, U.S., and EU.

The problem lies in the fact that the Ethiopian government was responsible for delivering the aid and in engaged in obstructionist and restrictive policies to block aid agencies from entering the stricken areas to conduct nutritional assessments. Ethiopian's closest ally, the United States, who would have had the strongest influence on the Ethiopian government, has actively ignored concerns about the distribution of food aid.

In 2009, atrocities against the Somalis in the Ogaden region continue unabated. The Ethiopian government formed a death squad consisting of 10,000 – 14,000 unemployed youths who were given the green light to do whatever they wanted in the Ogaden Region. These death squads were guilty of murder, rape torture, extrajudicial executions and detention of a massive number of people in desolate desert prisons. Women and children were subject to rape and sometimes imprisoned as sex slaves where they were victims of multiple rape and torture.

As well, the Ethiopian military carried out a scorched earth policy in which they burnt crops and homes, killed cattle and restricted access to water and other essential commodities. They burned eight villages and towns to the ground and killed many of the Somalis living there.

While the Ethiopian government were perpetrating these outrageous acts against the Somalis in the Ogaden region, the region suffered from the worst drought in 60 years. At the same time, the UN's World's Food Program (WFP) had been delivering aid directly to the Ethiopian military which then uses the aid to feed the paramilitary death squads who are committing atrocities in the region. (Thomas Mountain, *Feeding Death Squads*, Counterpunch, April 17, 2012) The largest donor was the United States which donated $847 million in assistance including $323 million in food aid.

Incredibly, while all these atrocities and natural disasters have been inflicted on the Ogaden people, the U.S., Britain and the World Bank, through a consortium known as the Development Assistance Group, had been donating huge sums of money to the Ethiopian government. This money was donated despite the fact that the government and the military were using the money in ways not intended by the donors.

United States donations in previous years were:

2004...............$402.03 million
2005...............$608.61 million
2006...............$315.78 million
2007...............$371.73 million
2008...............$811.37 million.

(Human Rights Watch, *Development Without Freedom: How Aid Underwrites Repression in Ethiopia*, October 2010)

Supporting a government whose human rights record is so unconscionable serves as proof that donors are only interested in the advantages which an Ethiopian ally can offer them. Human Rights Watch concludes that:

> Donor policy toward Ethiopia is shaped by at least two significant and interlinking factors. The first is the strategic position of Ethiopia in the Horn of Africa, which makes the country a key ally in the region for Western states seeking a bulwark against an intransigent Eritrea, an effective and radicalized insurgency in Somalia, and possible instability in neighboring Sudan following its referendum in 2011 [regarding the independence of Southern Sudan]. The second is the genuine, if exaggerated progress that Ethiopia has made to reduce poverty. (ibid)

Human Rights Watch then adds:

> But one would be mistaken to think that this aid is improving – or even having a neutral effect – on human rights in the country. The ruling EPRDF neither wants to discuss human rights concerns, nor allow donors to engage in or fund, independent programs that promote human rights and good governance. By quietly accepting the EPRDF's misuse of development assistance for partisan political purposes, donor countries are contributing to the oppression of Ethiopia's vulnerable populations. (ibid)

Another factor contributing to the ongoing support for Zenawi, in addition to the U.S. need for a surrogate army, was the need for sites for drone bases in strategic locations in order to fight its so-called meretricious war on terror.

East Africa is perceived to be a region in which al Qaeda and its affiliates are setting up shop due to the instability of the countries situated there and especially Somalia where al-Shabaab is fighting an insurgency against the U.S.-backed government. The Air Force has poured millions of tax payer dollars to upgrade the airport in Arba Minch, Ethiopia, so that it will become suitable as a drone base. A small annex already houses a fleet of drones that are reportedly only used for surveillance but can be equipped with Hellfire missiles and satellite-guided bombs.

According to a WikiLeaks document, drones launched from Ethiopia have already been armed with lethal missiles. Stratfor is a global intelligence company which provides confidential intelligence services to large corporations such as Dow Chemical Co., Lockheed Martin, Northrop Grumman and government agencies including the U.S. Department of Homeland security, the U.S. Marines and the U.S. Defence Intelligence Agency. According to an email sent from Stratfor:

> The Air Force has been secretly flying armed Reaper drones on counterterrorism missions from a remote civilian airport in southern Ethiopia as part of a rapidly expanding U.S.-led proxy war against an al-Qaeda affiliate in East Africa, U.S. military officials said.

(Wikileaks, Released on October 12, 2012)

According to an internal Stratfor document:

> A suspected U.S unmanned aerial vehicle late June 23 launched missiles against a jihadist camp in the small Somali coastal village of Khandal...reports from the village indicated...A Kismayo resident said the attack happened around 7 or 8 p.m. local time and resulted in many casualties, including members of the Islamic

militia al Shabaab in the area. (Stratfor, *Somalia: Explosions caused by Suspected U.S. Drone,* June 23, 2011)

Use of drones to kill alleged enemies violates international law including the UN Charter and the Geneva Conventions. Firing drones into a country where the United States is not at war violates Chapter 7, Article 51, of the UN charter thus constituting a war of aggression notwithstanding an authorization to use forces approved by Congress. The UN Charter is part of American law and an authorization to use force cannot violate international laws incorporated into the American legal system. On the other hand, people who are believed to be a threat to the security of the United States are entitled to due process irrespective of the suspicion of the danger they pose to U.S. security. According to the International Covenant for Civil and Political Rights:

Article 9. Everyone has the right to liberty and security of person. No one shall be subject to arbitrary arrest or detention.

Article 14. Everyone charged with a criminal offense shall have the right to be presumed innocent until proved guilty according to law.

Even when victims of drone attacks are highly suspected terrorists, they are denied their basic legal rights according to the above articles. If presumption of innocence is a tenet of law, then you cannot kill somebody without due process.

Tragically, many of those killed may have been chosen strictly on the basis of a pattern of behaviour known officially as a signature strike.

These victims are not only denied their basic legal rights but there is no real evidence to suspect them of any crime.

In addition, the habitually used justification "threat to the security of the United States" is so vague and amorphous that it opens the door to targeting people who are not guilty of any crime or certainly people who pose no threat to the security of the United States. Another reason to suspect the validity of the expression is its frivolous, excessive overexploitation whenever the U.S. government is trying to "manufacture consent" for the use of force. For example, Nicaragua, Guatemala, Panama, Dominican Republic, Grenada, Iraq and Afghanistan were at one time alleged threats to the security of the United States. The United States has cried "wolf" too often to be taken seriously.

One transcendent reason why drones are illegal is the fact that it is known that many innocent people are killed in drone attacks. It is inevitable that civilians will be killed given the indiscriminate nature of hellfire missiles which kill people in the vicinity of the alleged suspect. According to an exhaustive study undertaken by the Human Rights Clinic, Columbia University, "The Columbia Human Rights Clinic found reports of between 72 and 155 civilians killed in 2011 Pakistan drone strikes." Pakistan is only one of many countries where suspects are targeted with drone strikes. Killing innocent civilians violates the Geneva Conventions, the International Covenant for Civil and Political Rights, the Constitution of the World Health Organization, the International Covenant of Economic, Social and cultural Rights and the Universal Declaration of Human rights.

Furthermore, Ethiopia has become useful to the United States as a location for secret prisons for the interrogation and torture of prisoners. To maintain secrecy about the widespread use of torture and detaining prisoners without granting them their legal and civil rights, a network of secret prisons has been established to avoid public scrutiny and accountability. The Washington Post reports that:

> CIA and FBI agents hunting for al-Qaeda militants in the Horn of Africa have been interrogating terrorism suspects from 19 countries held in prisons in Ethiopia, which is notorious for torture and abuse...Human rights groups, lawyers and several Western diplomats assert hundreds of prisoners, who include women and children, have been transferred secretly and illegally in recent months from Kenya and Somalia to Ethiopia, where they are kept without charge or access to lawyers and families. (Anthony Mitchell, *U.S. Agents Visit Ethiopian Secret Jails*, The Washington Post, April 3, 2007)

Human Rights Watch reveals that:

> Those rendered were then transported to detention centers in Ethiopian capital Addis Ababa and other parts of Ethiopia, where they effectively disappeared. Denied access to their embassies, their families, and international humanitarian organizations such as the International Committee of the Red Cross (ICRC), the detainees were even denied phone calls home. Several detainees have said that they were housed in solitary-cells-some as small as two-by-two meters-with their hands cuffed in painful positions behind their backs and their feet bound together any time they were in their cells...Ethiopian security forces daily transported detainees-including several pregnant women-to a villa where US officials interrogated them. (Human Rights Watch, *Arrest, Detention, Rendition and Torture*, September 30, 2008)

Propping up Zenawi as President of Ethiopia has had another disastrous impact on the people of Ethiopia for which the American government must share complicity. Zenawi has invited foreign countries, who fear food shortages, to buy fertile land in Ethiopia at bargain basement prices, along with many incentives, to grow crops on that land for export back to their home country. The ramifications of this policy are the forced displacement of small farmers, food insecurity and a spike in food prices. According to the Oakland Institute:

> Since early 2008, the Ethiopian government has embarked on a process to award millions of hectares (ha) of land to foreign national agricultural investors. Our research shows that at least 3,619,509 ha of land have been transferred to investors, although the actual number may be higher. (Oakland Institute, *Understanding land investment deals in Africa*, 2011)

To purchase the land, investors sometimes pay as little as $1.10 per hectare, a steal by any standard. The Ethiopian government streamlined the purchasing process so that investors could purchase large plots of cheap fertile land without any obstacles and furthermore they have created a tax, regulatory and legal environment to entice foreign investors. Investors are provided with protections against investment risks.

Produce from this land is not meant for local consumption but is exported to countries such as India, Saudi Arabia, Cambodia and China. Local populations are never consulted about the sale of their land despite the fact that they are displaced from the land that belonged to them, sometimes with the use of force. The Oakland Institute points out that:

The Ethiopian government has used force and violence to silence dissent and compel acquiescence with the villagization program [forcing the farmers to live in villages]. According to Human Rights Watch, Ethiopian police have beaten and arrested those who question these policies, releasing them only on the condition that they support the program. (Oakland Institute, *Unheard Voices: The Human Rights Impact of Land Investments...*, 2013)

Farmers who once owned the land lost to foreign investors suffer on many fronts such as the loss of self-sufficiency, communal areas, ancestral lands, water and a clean environment. According to the Oakland Institute:

Taking over land and natural resources from rural Ethiopians, is resulting in a massive destruction of livelihoods and making millions of [farmers and pastoralists] dependent on food handouts. (Oakland Institute, *FAQs on Indian Investments in Ethiopia*, February 2013)

They also suffer from human right's abuses when they attempt to resist being evicted from their own land. Human Rights Watch reports that:

The Ethiopian government is forcibly moving tens of thousands of indigenous people in the western Gambella region from their homes to new villages under its "villagization" program. These population transfers are being carried out with no meaningful consultation and with no compensation. Despite government promises to provide basic resources and infrastructure, the new villages have inadequate food, agricultural support, and health and education facilities. Relocations have been marked by threats and assaults, and arbitrary arrest for those who resist the move. (Human Rights Watch, *Waiting for Death: Replacement and "Villagization" in Ethiopia's Gambella Region,* January 2012)

Ethiopia was already suffering from food shortages but the forced relocation of hundreds of thousands of indigenous people has severely exacerbated the problem. Ethiopia ranks at the bottom of the World Hunger Index reflecting the fact that between 12 and 15 million people in Ethiopia survive on food aid. Out of a population of 80 million people, 35 million people live in poverty. It also ranks 174th out of 187 on the UN Human Development Index.

Ethiopian served as a client state for the United States for a number of reasons, all for the benefit of the corporate and national security communities in the United States while the Ethiopian people and the people of the United States suffered as a result. Ethiopians suffered from lack of development, adequate assistance for famine relief, and from the brutality of the governments the United States maintained in power only because these governments were subservient to their masters in Washington. Americans suffered due to the greatly elevated risk from terrorism and from the misplaced spending priorities of their government that chose to waste money protecting the rapacious economic interests of the few rather than spending on the desperate needs of the many.

CHAPTER 5

Rwanda/Uganda

Ranked as one of the great human rights tragedies since World War II, the Rwandan genocide is commonly understood in the context of a tribal internecine conflict between the Hutus and Tutsis. The event that triggered the genocide is imputed to the shooting down of a plane carrying the President of Rwanda and Burundi, responsibility for which has been attributed to Paul Kagame, current President of Rwanda.

Escaping culpability in the media and public consciousness for the genocide, Bill Clinton and others at the highest levels of the U.S. government, United Nations, France, Britain, Belgium and others share responsibility and possibly complicity for the genocide which left 800,000 dead in its wake.

In this chapter, I will examine the events leading up to and including the genocide and U.S. involvement in those events followed by an analysis of Clinton's possible complicity in that genocide. In addition, I will examine the role of Uganda in the civil war in Rwanda and the American use of Uganda as a surrogate force in Africa.

Tension in Rwanda between the Tutsis and Hutus really began during colonial times in 1959. When the Hutus seized power from the Tutsis who had been maintained in power by Belgium, hatred between the two tribes intensified. Hutu politicians set out to demonize the Tutsi population by revising history to depict the Tutsi as foreign invaders who had enslaved the Hutu population. Their motive was to perpetuate power for the Hutus in order to be the sole beneficiaries of the wealth of Rwanda and to reclaim control of the country they believed was usurped by the minority Tutsis.

Hutu resentment of Belgium-backed Tutsi power fomented resentment in the Hutu majority who formed the emancipation party, Parmehutu, in 1957, led by Gregoire Kayibanda. As a reaction to the Hutu party, the Tutsis formed the UNAR party in 1957 which supported the Tutsi monarchy and quickly became militarized. After the creation of an independent Rwanda in 1962, Kayibanda served as president from 1962 to July 5, 1973.

In November 1959, a Tutsis assault on a Hutu official provoked reprisals including attacks on Tutsi officials, but when the Tutsis responded with more violence, Belgium intervened to restore order and replaced about half of the Tutsi local authorities with Hutus.

When clashes between Hutus and Tutsis erupted again, 10,000 Tutsis were killed and approximately 200,000 were forced to leave the country.

A vote was held in September 1961, and 80% of Rwandans supported an end to the Tutsi monarchy and the establishment of a republic. Some of the Tutsi exiles living in Uganda formed small insurgent groups and repeatedly led attacks against Hutus in Rwanda in the hope of restoring Tutsi power. These attacks incited Hutus to exact revenge on Tutsis still living there. As a harbinger of the 1994 Genocide, Hutu vigilante groups armed with machetes, spears and clubs set out to kill every Tutsi in sight with a death toll of 5,000 and external displacement of another 200,000 Tutsis. These clashes became an ongoing reciprocity of violence thus planting the seeds that would be reaped in 1994.

Kayibunda intensified the animus between the two groups by launching a round of repression against the Tutsis in the hope of uniting the Hutus behind him. In 1972, Kayibanda ordered vigilante groups to restrict Tutsi admission to schools, the University, civil service and every sector of employment to nine percent. Whereas Tutsis constituted 30% of the population, the restrictions resulted in another mass exodus of Tutsis.

Nevertheless, Kayibanda's hate campaign was not sufficient to save his presidency due to his neglect of northern Hutus by not employing them in his government. As a result, in 1973, Karibanda became the victim of a military coup led by General Juvénal Habyarimana, a northerner.

Habyarimana established a one party dictatorship subjecting the population to harsher restrictions forcing everyone to carry an identity card specifying their ethnic group and their place of residence. Changing residences was only permissible with official approval. He also continued to enforce the restrictions implemented by Kayibanda.

Two years after the coup, Habyarimana officially established Rwanda as a one-party state under Habyarimana known as the National Revolutionary Movement for Development (MRND). MRND was the only legal political party in the country from 1975 until 1991 and every Rwandan was automatically a member of the party.

Despite his exercise of strict political control, Habyarimana was determined to improve the standard of living for some Rwandans by improving the infrastructure and developing the economy. During the 1970s and 1980s, he attracted substantial foreign aid which was used to build roads, telephones and electric service. Although some people became wealthy during this period, the majority of the population remained poor as more than 90% of the population depended on agriculture to survive.

A sharp blow was dealt to the economy when coffee, responsible for 75% of Rwanda's foreign exchange, dropped drastically in price forcing the government to borrow money from the World Bank. The international banks are controlled by Europe, North America and Japan through a skewed voting system and thus serve these countries' interests. In order to qualify for loans, developing countries must accept conditions that force these countries' to adopt neoliberal policies and adopt other measures that give wealthy countries an economic or trade advantage.

The growing imbalance of wealth not only bifurcated the population on the basis of wealth but also on the basis of tribe. Habyarimana responded to the crisis by creating a system of quotas which were ostensibly designed to ensure an equitable division of wealth and opportunities for all Rwandans but in fact restricted access of Tutsis to education and employment.

Economic decline, increasing corruption and favoritism on the part of Habyarimana induced journalists, political leaders and intellectuals to demand reforms to the political and economic system. In 1990, Habyarimana reacted by appointing a national commission to examine the issues responsible for the crisis.

While Habyarimana was addressing problems in Rwanda and favoring northern Hutus in the process, important events were occurring in Uganda involving Tutsi refugees which would later have a critical impact on the destiny of Rwanda.

When Milton Obote, President of Uganda in his second term from 1980 to 1985, was persecuting the Tutsis and Tutsi-related groups in 1983, hundreds of young Tutsis joined Yoweri Museveni's southern-based National Resistance Army (NRA) whose purpose was to win control of Uganda. Two of the Tutsis who joined the NRA were Paul Kagame who had escaped Hutu repression in Rwanda and General Fred Rwigyema, also a Tutsi exile from Rwanda.

By the time Museveni and the NRA conquered Kampala, in January 1986, one-quarter of his army -3000 men- were Tutsi fighters, the sons of Rwandan exiles. Even more Tutsis joined the NRA and Museveni declared that all Rwanda exiles who had lived in Uganda for more than ten years were automatically citizens. On the other hand, Tutsi exiles campaigned for the right-of-return to Rwanda. Leading exiles formed the Rwanda Patriotic Front (RPF) to support political reform in Rwanda or failing that, to take Rwanda by force.

When news spread from Rwanda that Habyarimana was teetering on the brink of collapse, Rwigyema decided that the time was ripe for an invasion of Rwanda and overnight 4,000 Tutsi soldiers deserted the Ugandan army to join forces with the Rwandan Patriotic Army (RPA), the military wing of the RPF.

The invasion in October 1990 was a disaster and Rwigema was killed on the second day. One of the major causes of early defeats of the RPA was the intervention of French troops who accepted Habyarimana's argument that the real purpose of the invasion was to establish Tutsi rule. President Mitterrand, a friend of Habyarimana, quickly dispatched French troops to Rwanda. To dramatize the urgency of French intervention, Habyarimana arranged for a staged attack on Kigali. France sent more troops and drove the rebels across the border.

With French assistance, Habyarimana set in motion a huge buildup of Rwanda's armed forces from a force of 9,000 men on October 1, 1990, to 28,000 in 1991.

Under pressure from Western donors and local politicians, Habyarimana relented and agreed to set up a multi-party state. In June 1991, he passed a constitutional amendment granting legal status to opposition parties. By April 1992, he formed a coalition government with some of the opposition parties.

At the same time, Habyarimana extended an olive branch to the RPF for the purpose of negotiating a ceasefire. At the end of 1991, Kagame became the leader of the RPA and transformed it into a disciplined guerilla force of 5,000 soldiers capable of staging hit-and-run raids on Rwanda. Between 1990 and 1993, the RPA launched numerous guerilla attacks in Rwanda plunging the country into civil war.

For their part, Hutus inflamed the growing conflagration of hatred by murdering innocent Tutsis inside Rwanda. For example, Hutus slaughtered 300 Tutsi civilians in Kabirira in October 1990; in January 1991, 500 to 1,000 Tutsis were murdered in Kinigi; Hutu militias in Bugesera massacred 300 Tutsis. Human Rights watch concluded that between 1991 and 1993, paramilitary groups working with the government as well as government soldiers killed an estimated 2,000 non-combatant civilians. Most of the victims were Tutsi.

Rwandan military and police forces detained hundreds of people in military camps, many of whom were beaten and tortured while a number were killed. In Kigali alone, 8,000 people, mostly Tutsis, were detained without charges and beaten and tortured. Rwandan soldiers looted and raped throughout Rwanda with impunity and removed thousands of civilians from their homes.

Tragically, there were many countries that were willing to supply arms to the different parties in the conflict exponentially facilitating their capability to murder more innocent civilians. Uganda was one of the main suppliers to the RPF, giving them a steady supply of small arms, ammunition, food, gasoline Kalashnikov rifles. According to Human Rights Watch:

> The arms project finds a high degree of institutional complicity between the NRA
> and the RPF. At the very least, Uganda and its leaders are responsible for allowing
> military renegades to plan and execute the invasion of a sovereign state with

Uganda weapons, launched from Uganda...There is credible evidence that the Ugandan government allowed RPF to move arms, logistical supplies and troops across Ugandan soil, and provided direct military support in the form of arms, ammunition, and military equipment. (Human Rights Watch, Arming Rwanda and Human Rights Abuses in the Rwandan War, January 1, 1994, DOC A601)

It is important to bear in mind that Uganda was a close ally of the United States and often served as a proxy army for the Pentagon. Both the United States and the World Bank provided Museveni with the funds for buying large quantities of weapons and ammunition.

As an ally of the United States, Uganda allowed the basing of American drones in Uganda for surveillance of neighboring countries. In June, 2011, the U.S proposed to spend $145.4 million on the War on Terror in East Africa which included four Raven systems (a type of Drone) to be used by forces from Uganda to Burundi.

In addition, Uganda served as an ideal place for the location of black sites (secret prisons) for the detention mainly of Kenyans and Somalis to fight the War on Terror. According to Reuters:

Rights groups say 13 Kenyans have been seized and illegally transferred to neighboring Uganda, where they have been denied proper access to legal representation and grilled by agents from the Federal Bureau of Investigation. (Richard Lough, *Analysis: Kenya renditions raise U.S. proxy detention questions, Business & Financial News*, October 18, 2010)

U.S. Military aid to Uganda at a time when Museveni was perpetrating genocide against the Acholi people living in Northern Uganda renders the United States complicit in the genocide. According to the Convention on the Prevention and Punishment of the Crime of Genocide, Article 3:

The following acts shall be punishable:
(a) Genocide;
(b) Conspiracy to commit genocide;
(c) Direct and public incitement to commit genocide;
(d) Attempt to commit genocide;
(e) Complicity in genocide.

By providing arms to a country with the knowledge that the country is intentionally committing genocide makes the United States guilty of conspiracy or complicity in genocide.

People in Northern Uganda suffered gruesome treatment by Uganda Peoples' Defence Forces (UPDF), the Ugandan army, and the Lord's Resistance Army (LRA) who are a group of soldiers originally from the government which was deposed by Museveni.

Forced displacement of the Acholi people began in 1996 and was partly motivated by the rapacious allurement of fertile land for large-scale farming. Over 90 percent of the Acholi population, or 1.6 million people, were rounded up and forced to live in the most sordid conditions in squalid, wretched concentration camps where guards would regularly torture, kill, rape and mutilate the inmates. The World Health Organization reported that over 1,000 people die each week of starvation and preventable diseases. Young Acholi boys and girls were recruited by Museveni to serve as child soldiers in the UPDF. Human Rights Watch reports that:

The government remains responsible for many of the hardships endured by the displaced population. Since 1996 the government has used the army to undertake a massive forced displacement of the population...Many of those displaced including almost the entire population of the three Acholi districts live in squalid conditions in displaced persons camps that are susceptible to LRA attacks. The Ugandan army has failed to protect these camps compounding the harm inflicted by the original forced displacement.

(Human Rights Watch, *Uprooted and Forgotten: Impunity and Human Rights Abuses in Northern Uganda*, Vol. 17 No. 12(A), September 2005)

Other motives for the relocation of the Acholi people included carrying out "the classic counter-insurgency strategy of 'draining the sea' – removing the population from the rural areas in which the rebels operate" (ibid) and the eventual discovery of oil in the region. The New York Times reveals that:

The recent discovery of large reserves of oil – estimated to be at least 2.5 billion barrels – could turn Uganda into a major player in Africa. The expected revenue of up to $2 billion a year has the potential to propel Uganda into the strata of middle-income countries, where few sub-Saharan countries rank. A refinery will be built; infrastructure is promised. (The New York Times/International Herald Tribune, Global edition, *Uganda*, August 3 2012)

The rebel militia, LRA, inflicted similar atrocities on the people of Northern Uganda. Museveni speciously claimed that his justification for detaining people in Northern Uganda was to protect the Acholi people from the LRA but their treatment by his soldiers belies his defence of his actions.

Origins of the LRA resulted from Museveni's overthrow of his predecessor, General Okello, and his usurping of the presidency of Uganda. Museveni sought vengeance against the people of Northern Uganda by committing atrocities such as burning, looting, rape, killing and torture.

His treatment of Northern Ugandans spawned a resistance movement led by Alice Lakwena who believed she was inspired by the Holy Spirit of God and was thus a prophet. Joseph Kony formed another resistance group but took a page from Lakwena's book and considered himself a prophet as well. When Lakwena's group was defeated by Museveni, her followers were recruited by Kony. In 1987, Kony's militia, now known as the LRA, consisted mostly of Acholi people.

During much of the 1990s, the LRA was based in Southern Sudan where they received funding from the Sudanese government in revenge for Museveni's funding of the Sudan People's Liberation Movement (SPLM), a rebel group in Sudan.

Kony returned to Northern Uganda to wreak havoc on the Acholi people and also engaged in battle against the UPDF. In one area alone, Makombo, the LRA killed more than 321 people and abducted 250 more including at least 80 children. Adult men were tied up and hacked to death with machetes or had their skulls crushed with axes. Children were raped and recruited as soldiers. Human Rights Watch reveals that:

> The LRA used similar tactics in each village they attacked during their four-day operation. Those who were abducted, including many children aged 10 to 15 years

old, were tied up with ropes or metal wire, often in human chains of 5 to 15 people. They were made to carry the goods the LRA had pillaged and then forced to march off with them. Anyone who refused, walked too slowly, or who tried to escape was killed. (Human Rights Watch, *Trail of Death*, March 28 2010)

Despite the horrific fate suffered by the Acholi at the hands of the UPDF and Kony's LRA, Western governments refused to accept refugees from Northern Uganda, maintaining that Museveni 's government was democratic. A study undertaken by the Centre for Refugee Studies at York and Queen's Universities discloses that:

Those who escaped persecution from Acholiland are often denied asylum by democratic and industrialized governments, especially Canada, Sweden, Norway, the United Kingdom and the United States. Contrary to overwhelming evidence, governments of these states maintain that the Museveni regime is democratic, protects and enhances human rights, and provides peace, stability and protection to the people in Acholiland. (Ogenga Otunnu, *The Path to Genocide in Northern Uganda*, Refuge VOL. 17 No. 3, August 1998)

The same attitude prevails today as reflected in statements by Barack Obama related to his decision to deploy 100 troops in Northern Uganda when he claimed that:

Deploying these U.S. Armed Forces furthers U.S. national security interests and foreign policy and will be a significant contribution toward counter-LRA efforts in central Africa...Although the U.S. forces are combat-equipped, they will only be providing information, advice, and assistance to partner nation forces, and they will not themselves engage LRA forces unless necessary for self-defense..

(Jake Tapper and Luis Martinez, *Obama Sends 100 US Troops to Uganda to Help Combat Lord's Resistance Army*, ABC News, October 14 2011)

An analysis of Obama's statements reveals that he considers Museveni a friend despite his war crimes in Northern Uganda which vary negligibly from those of Kony. Promising that U.S. Armed Forces will only advise and collect information defies almost every historical precedent. The question then arises of what exactly did Obama imply by "national security"? Neither Uganda nor the LRA pose a threat to the U.S. unless Obama is referring to the secret prisons and drones located in Uganda which could be subject to a threat from a rebel group. Nevertheless, the use of "national security" as a justification is just another example of meretricious hyperbole.

Meanwhile, in Rwanda, in July 1992, a ceasefire was agreed upon and Habyarimana agreed to participate in peace talks in Arusha, Tanzania, with the RPF. Signed on August 4 1993, the Accords called for a ceasefire, a power-sharing arrangement, and return to multi-party rule. It formally ended the war and established steps for reconciliation including power-sharing through the creation of a new transitional government in which all parties would be fairly represented. As well, the accords called for the integration of both armies into a single national army and the right-of-return of all Rwandan refugees.

To monitor and assist in the implementation of this agreement, the United Nations passed UN Resolution 872 on October 5 1993 which created a Chapter VI peacekeeping mission, known as the United Nations Assistance Mission for Rwanda (UNAMIR) with a mandate to monitor the ceasefire agreement, to establish an expanded demilitarized zone, to neutralize armed gangs and to demobilize militias. The authorized strength of UNAMIR was 2,500 troops. Ultimately, the mission lacked the resources and support from the Security Council to be effective reflecting the indifference of the major nations on the council in strengthening the UN force in Rwanda. Each country had their own motives such as France who was arming Habyarimana and the United States whose objectives will be examined in great detail later.

To weaken the fragile line between a tentative peace and all-out-conflict, Habyarimana distributed nearly 2,000 assault rifles to civilians loyal to the MRND. In addition, a number of foreign sources flooded both sides in Rwanda with weapons which, according to Human Rights Watch, contributed to "an unprecedented accumulation of a wide variety of arms, including the introduction of heavier, long-range weapons systems." Human Rights watch summarizes the weapons accumulation as:

1. Six million dollars in arms sales from Egypt;
2. France offered a bank guarantee of $6 million for arms purchases;
3. South Africa sold $5.9 million in arms purchases;
4. Uganda provided weapons, munitions, automatic rifles and mortars;
5. United States military sales to Rwanda totalled $2.3 million. (ibid)

Rapprochement with the RPG and the new coalition government enraged Hutu supremacists who would not settle for anything less than eradicating the country of all Tutsis and moderate Hutus who were willing to compromise with the RPF. These supremacists formed a network of police, members of the army and the administration to promote the cause of Hutu power. A militant youth wing of the MRND formed a youth militia called the Interahamwe (those who work or fight together). Unemployed youths were easily recruited by the Interahamwe with the promise of jobs and other rewards.

The plethora of unemployed youths hid a deeper problem involving international banks whose impact on Rwanda was very nefarious. For example, Michel Chossudovsky claims that:

> The civil war was preceded by the flare-up of a deep-seated economic crisis. It was the restructuring of the agricultural system under IMF-World Bank supervision which precipitated the population into abject poverty and destitution. The deterioration of the economic environment, which immediately followed the collapse of the international coffee market...exacerbated simmering ethnic tensions and accelerated the process of political collapse. (Michel Chossudovsky, *The Globalization of poverty and the New World Order,* Global Research, 1997)

A large share of national income and government revenues depended on coffee thereby affecting the level of unemployment. Huge debts to the World Bank and IMF are always accompanied by strict conditions which basically forced the government to adopt neoliberal economic policies. IMF conditionalities forced the Rwanda government to implement a 50% reduction in the value of the Rwandan franc which led to a spike in inflation. A second devaluation led to the tumbling of coffee production and the small income derived from coffee had been erased with nothing to serve as a substitute. The collapse in the coffee market led to a swelling of the unemployed serving as a source of recruits for the Interhamwe.

Western embassies recognized that the Interahamwe were a dangerous group whose mission was to exterminate the entire Tutsi population and Hutus who were considered moderate because they supported a coalition government with the Tutsis. Western governments had clear and obvious indications that the Interhamwe were preparing for a slaughter of Tutsis and moderate Hutus from warnings of their own officials and from Romeo Dallaire, the head of the military wing of UNAMIR. In particular, after the genocide was underway, the vociferous exhortations from various officials seemed to fall on deaf ears.

According to Gregory H. Stanton, Professor of Genocide Studies at George Mason University in Virginia, "The U.S. government was forewarned of the impending genocide. Communications were sent by cable, email, and secure telephone from the U.S. embassy in Kigali informing the State Department about general Dallaire's premonitions months before April 6." (Gregory H. Stanton, *The Rwandan Genocide: Why Early Warning Failed*, Journal of African Conflicts and Peace Studies, VOL 1 Number 2, September 2009) As well, Stanton reports that, "Although the U.S. Defense Agency recognized from radio intercepts as early as April 7 that centrally organized mass killings of Tutsis was underway, D.I.A. warnings went unheeded in the American government." (ibid) In addition, he reveals that, "The U.S. Embassy's Deputy Chief of Mission Joyce Leader has told me personally that she began using the word genocide in her daily telephone calls to the State Department from the start.". (Human Rights Watch, *Arming Rwanda and Human Rights Abuses in the Rwandan War*, January 1, 1994, DOC A601)

In case there was any doubt about the intentions of the extremists in the Habyarimana's government and the Interhamwe, Dallaire sent a fax to Major Maurice Baril, UN Secretary-General's military advisor reporting that an informant who was a high official in Habyarimana's government had revealed that there was a plan to exterminate the Tutsis.

As you will discover in the second part of this chapter, President Clinton did everything within his power to stop or delay the United Nations from sending a 5,000 Chapter VII peacekeeping mission which according to a number of experts would have stopped the genocide in its tracks.

Between January 1993 and March 1994, Rwanda imported more than 500,000 machetes, the weapon of choice during the genocide. The International Development Association (IDA), an affiliate of the World Bank, the African Development Fund (ADF), the European Development Fund (EDF), Germany, Belgium, Canada and the United States were guilty of diverting funds targeted for development into funding the Rwandan military and the Interhamwe. Shockingly, Habyarimana used World Bank Money to finance the import of machetes. (Michel Chossudovsky, *The Globalization of Poverty and the New World Order*, Global Research, 1997) By the end of 1993, there were caches of firearms, machetes and axes throughout Rwanda in preparation for the genocide.

At the same time as they were stockpiling weapons, the Interhamwe were training and recruiting more members for the extermination of Tutsis. To be capable of identifying the targeted population quickly, the Interhamwe created lists of Tutsis and moderate Hutus. As well, Interhamwe recruits had been organized into units of 40 and dispersed throughout Kigali.

Throughout the preparatory stages of the genocide, the plotters attempted to foment anger, hate and vengeance against the Tutsis. Radio broadcasts were laced with inflammatory speeches in which the Tutsis were demonized and blamed for all the ills of Rwanda. Many broadcasts pointed to the invasion of the RPF blaming all Tutsis in Rwanda for the invasion and calling for their slaughter.

Public rallies were another means of spreading propaganda and inciting violence to prepare the Hutu majority to at least accept the slaughter of all Tutsis.

Habyarimana delayed the transition to an interim government which had been originally scheduled for January 1994 through specious interpretations of the Arusha Accords. The extremist Hutus within his government had no intention of relinquishing power to an interim government in which Tutsis shared power with the Hutus.

Pressure was mounting on all sides on Habyarimana from Western and African governments who were demanding the implementation of the Arusha accords and from the extremists in his own party who were angry that he had signed the Accords.

On April 6 1994, Habyarimana attended a one-day summit meeting with African leaders in Dares Salaam, Tanzania, where he was subjected to a barrage of criticism for not adhering to the schedule in the Accords. On the return flight, April 6, to Kigali, Habyarimana was accompanied by Burundi president, Cyprien Ntariamira. Two missiles struck the plane killing all aboard. Responsibility for the attack is in dispute with some blaming the RPG and others blaming the extremist Hutus in the Habyarimana government. In January 2012, a French investigation confirmed that the missile was fired from a military camp and not from the Tutsis. (Washington Post, *French Probe find missile fire from military camp downed Rwanda president's plane in 1994*, January 11, 2012)

Irrespective of who was responsible, the incident was the trigger that set off the genocide. The Interhamwe set up road blocks across Rwanda to prevent any Tutsis from leaving the country. Tutsis were in a prison from which there was no escape and where they were sitting on a time-bomb slated to be killed. At the centre of the planned assassinations was Colonel Bagosoro, chief of staff in Habyarimana's defense ministry, who assumed power and immediately ordered the implementation of the plans to eliminate all Tutsis in Rwanda.

Victims had already been carefully selected and soldiers from the presidential guard and interhamwe militiamen hunted down prominent Hutus - politicians, senior government officials, lawyers, teachers, human rights activists and independent journalists - who were all considered opponents of the mass massacre of Tutsis.

Gangs armed with clubs, machetes and knives went from door to door searching for Tutsi victims. Roadblocks had been set up by militiamen demanding identity cards and killing Tutsis on the spot. Massacres followed in quick succession not only in Tutsi homes but in churches. In one church during a mass for 500 Tutsis, a killing squad burst into the church and began slashing away with machetes. The killing endured for two hours. Incredibly, one girl survived by hiding under other bodies covered with their blood giving the impression that she was already dead. She remained there until the killing was over and for many hours after the killers departed.

Death by the killers was brutal and macabre due to their heinous methods which included slicing open peoples' bellies or grabbing young children by the feet and slamming them against trees. Bodies began to pile up everywhere as over 10,000 people were slaughtered every day. According to the United Nations, 800,000 people died during the genocide which lasted 100 days, destroying about ¾ of the Tutsi population. The crime, as discussed below, meets the standards of the genocide convention.

During the massacre of Tutsis, the civil war against the RPF raged on until July 4, 1994, at which time the RPF gained control of Kigali. RPF forces immediately advanced on HUTU strongholds forcing about 100,000 of the Interhamwe to seek refuge across the border in Zaire (formerly the Democratic Republic of the Congo). During the genocide, an estimated 900,000 Tutsis and moderate Hutus had also sought refuge in Zaire and Tanzania.

On July 18, once the Hutu stronghold had been destroyed, Kagame declared that the civil war was over and formed a government of national unity comprising all parties except the MRND which he banned. Political organizing was banned until 2003. Paul Kagame was appointed Vice-President and minister of Defence in the Government of National Unity on July 19, 1994.

The entire country had been ravaged including hospitals, schools and churches. Government offices had been looted; police were non-existent; the treasury was empty; public utilities had collapsed and a year's harvest had been lost. Ditches and churches were filled with rotting bodies and nearly two million people had been uprooted from their homes. On April 22, 2000, Kagame took the oath as President of the Republic of Rwanda after being elected by the Transitional National Assembly. Rwanda's election in 2003 was the country's first popular vote for president since the genocide. Prior to the election, Rwandan voters supported a new constitution designed to prevent another genocide through a reorganization of legislative bodies and political guidelines for political administrations. The presidential term was limited to seven years. Kagame was elected to a second term in 2010 but not without controversy. Electoral victory for Kagame was marred by violence including the killing of potential opponents. In addition, newspapers and radio stations had been shut down.

On the other hand, during Kagame's tenure leading up to the 2010 election, Rwanda enjoyed high rates of growth, improvements to infrastructure, an increase in foreign investment and tourism.

One important issue which has been virtually ignored was the role played by the Clinton Administration during the genocide. Although the U.S. has been criticized for its lack of action before and during the slaughter, the depth of Clinton's complicity in the genocide has been neglected.

President Clinton's remark in Rwanda after the killing had ended that "Never again must we be shy in the face of the evidence" is hypocritical in the extreme. His hypocrisy lies in the fact that the U.S. government was principally responsible for the initial withdrawal of UN peacekeeping troops from Rwanda who were desperately needed to halt the killing. He also delayed a second peacekeeping mission which would have halted the slaughter. Such actions violate the Genocide Convention and in particular, Article 1, which obliges states to use all means at their disposal to prevent genocide.

Before examining my claim that Clinton was complicit in the genocide, it is essential to examine the meaning of "complicity" and also the obligation of states to prevent genocide as stated in Article 1 of the Genocide Convention.

There are two levels of guilt defined in the Genocide Convention, the more serious of which is direct guilt and the other is complicity in genocide. Two types of actions with respect to guilt in genocide are implied by the Convention; an act of commission and an act of omission, the former referring to direct participation of a state in genocide while the latter refers to failure of a state to meet its obligations to prevent genocide.

In order to be complicit in genocide, a number of criteria must be met. Complicit in genocide requires that the genocide itself must satisfy all the conditions set out in the Genocide Convention. In the case of Rwanda, there is a general consensus among scholars and the United Nations that the slaughter of Tutsis and moderate Hutus constituted genocide. According to Samantha Power who teaches human rights and U.S. foreign policy at Harvard's John F. Kennedy School of Government, "The case for a label of genocide was the most straightforward since the Holocaust".

Additionally, to be complicit entails knowledge of the genocidal intent of the perpetrators. It will be demonstrated later in this chapter that President Clinton did have this knowledge.

The scope of complicity has been expanded through a ruling of the International Criminal Court for the Former Yugoslavia on December 10, 1998, which stated that: "Encouragement given to the perpetrators may be punishable, even if the abettor did not take any tangible action, provided it 'directly and substantially' assists in the commission of a crime." Interpreting the ruling, a passage from the International Law Commission's Commentary reaches the conclusion that "Action could include aiding or abetting...Indeed the word 'abet' includes mere exhortation or encouragement." Further discussion of Clinton's encouragement of the extreme Hutus will be discussed later.

The Genocide Convention defines the obligation to prevent and punish genocide in Article 1 which states that, "The contracting Parties confirm that genocide, whether committed in time of peace or in time of war, is a crime under international law which they undertake to prevent and to punish" and Article VIII which states that, "Any contracting party may call upon the competent organs of the United Nations to take such action under the Charter of the United Nations as they consider appropriate for the prevention and suppression of acts of genocide."

To clarify and specify the precise meaning of these Articles, I will refer to a February 27, 2007 ruling of the International Criminal Court in the case of Bosnia and Herzegovina vs. Serbia and Montenegro. In paragraph 430 of the ruling, it states that, "Responsibility [for genocide] is however incurred if the state manifestly failed to take all measures to prevent genocide which were within its power, and which might have contributed to preventing the genocide." In addition, the ruling states in paragraph 431 that, "In fact, a State's obligation to prevent, and the corresponding duty to act, arise at the instant that the State learns of, or should normally have learned of, the serious risk that genocide will be committed." Note that the leaders of a State cannot plead ignorance if their intelligence, State Department and security agencies had full knowledge of the genocide because the assumption in these circumstances is that the leader would have known or normally should have known about the genocide.

I shall prove that not only did the United States fail to act on its own or collectively with other states but deliberately took actions to prevent the United Nations from acting on a number of different occasions or to undermine operations already underway. The U.S. pressured the Security Council into reducing its peacekeeping force to an inefficacious number of troops, eschewing the use of the word "genocide" to abrogate the legal obligation to act under the Genocide Convention, perniciously limiting the scope of the mandate of a second UN mission, delaying the vote on a resolution to expand UN peacekeeping forces in Rwanda, and refusing to fund or contribute necessary supplies once the resolution passed.

In fact, all these actions of the U.S. did have a significant impact on the prosecution of the genocide. A study undertaken by the Carnegie Institute in 1997 reported that "In the midst of the slaughter,...Major Romeo Dallaire of Canada, maintained that a capable force inserted within two weeks after the death of the presidents could have stopped much of the killing...In his assessment, 5,000 troops operating under a peace enforcement mission...could have prevented massive violence; and assisted in the return of refugees and displaced persons." The Carnegie Report then concluded that, "The Carnegie Institute, The Institute for the Study of Diplomacy at Georgetown University, and the United States Army convened a panel of senior military leaders to...assess the validity of General Dallaire's claims. The panel generally agreed that early military intervention – within two weeks of the initial violence – by a force of 5,000 could have made a significant difference in the level of violence."

First appearing in Rwanda in October 1993, a UN peacekeeping mission named "The UN Assistance Mission for Rwanda" (UNAMIR) was authorized as a Chapter VI operation by UN Resolution 872 after the second invasion of Rwanda by the RPF in February of the same year. Chapter VI missions authorize peacekeepers to maintain peace and restore order through diplomatic measures while Chapter VII authorizes missions to use force if necessary.

An important issue in assessing whether or not former President Clinton shares complicity in the Rwandan genocide is the question of when and how much knowledge did he have about the slaughter of Tutsis and moderate Hutus. State Department and Intelligence documents were circulated on a daily basis to the President and senior officials in his administration referring to the genocide in Rwanda. For example, on April 23, 1994, just 17 days after the initial killing, a CIA daily briefing stated that, "They (RPF) may be willing to meet the military officers and political leaders, however, in an effort to stop the genocide." Another daily intelligence briefing from the Secretary of state, Warren Christopher, on April 26, 1994, calls attention to, "The

Red Cross Estimate that 100,000 to 500,000 people, mostly Tutsis, have been killed in Rwanda's ethnic bloodletting."

Not only did Clinton know about the genocide, he was either aware or should reasonably have been aware of the genocidal intentions of the extreme Hutus. Anthony Lake, who had been Deputy Assistant Secretary of State for African Affairs, revealed later that "The U.S. government knew 'within 10 to 14 days' of the plane crash that the slaughter was 'premeditated, carefully planned, was being executed according to plan with the full connivance of the then-Rwandan government'."

UNAMIR peacekeepers numbered approximately 2,500 before April 26, 1994, but pressure from United States forced the Security Council to downsize the force to 270 troops. The United States was determined to obviate any real or perceived obligation to send American troops to Rwanda. Somalia had chilled American willingness to send troops for peacekeeping missions since, at that time, 19 Americans were killed and one was dragged around the streets of Mogadishu for all to see on American network television. Several policies were contrived to ensure American avoidance of the need to intervene, one of which was to withdraw all peacekeepers from Rwanda and the other was to circumvent calling the massacre "genocide".

Removing UN troops from Rwanda played into the hands of the extreme Hutus whose mission was not to share power with the Tutsis but to exterminate them. To discourage nations from participating in UN peacekeeping, the extremists killed 10 Belgium troops provoking Belgium into withdrawing their peacekeepers from Rwanda.

To reduce UNAMIR to a token force, senior American officials issued orders to the U.S. mission at the United Nations to press for UNAMIR withdrawal. For example, a note from the Secretary of State, Warren Christopher, to Madeline Albright, in April 94 stated that, "Taking these factors into account [the] Department believes that there is insufficient justification to retain a UN peacekeeping presence in Rwanda...USUN is instructed to inform NSC colleagues that the United States believes that the first priority of the Security Council is to instruct the Secretary- General to implement an orderly withdrawal of all UNAMIR forces from Rwanda." In addition, on April 13, 1994, Assistant Secretary of State for International Organizations, Douglas J. Bennet, advised the Secretary of State that, "Given the chaotic conditions in Rwanda, it is impossible for UNAMIR to fulfill its mandate. It is our view, therefore, that the force should withdraw from the country now."

Notwithstanding that senior members of the administration already knew that genocide was occurring in Rwanda, they carefully avoided the use of the term publicly to establish that the imperative in the Convention to act did not apply. This would protect the government from accusations that the U.S. stood by during the commission of genocide. On May 1, 1994, a discussion paper from the Office of the Secretary of Defense warns that, "Language that calls for an international investigation of human rights abuses and possible violations of the genocide Convention...could commit the USG to actually 'do something'." As well, in a cable sent from the U.S. Mission at the U.N. to Secretary of state Warren Christopher on April 27, 1994, a senior official warned that "The events in Rwanda clearly seem to meet the definition of Genocide in Article II of the 1948 Convention...However, if the council acknowledges that, it may be forced to 'take such action under the charter as they consider appropriate for the prevention and suppression of acts of genocide' as provided for in Article VIII."

The UN decision to withdraw UNAMIR troops under pressure from the United States encouraged the Hutu extremists to accelerate the killing. Samantha Power understood that the, "Hutu were generally reluctant to massacre large groups of Tutsis if foreigners (armed or unarmed) were present...It did not take many UN soldiers to dissuade the Hutu from attacking." Also, the Physicians for Human Rights claim that, "In the days following the April 21 decision to reduce UNAMIR forces, mass killings skyrocketed." (Physicians for Human Rights, *The 1994 Genocide and U.S. Policy*, p. 2)

Secretary General, Boutros Boutros-Ghali was under pressure from a few non-permanent members of the Security Council to urge African nations to contribute troops for a new peacekeeping mission. American leadership, fearing a successful campaign to create a new peacekeeping mission for Rwanda, established an interagency process to produce a Presidential Directive which would include severely prohibitive criteria for deploying UN troops and to define strict rules of engagement.

On May 6, 1994, the White House released PDD-25, signed by President Clinton, in which the central principle of U.S. peacekeeping participation was defined as, "Peace operations are not and cannot be the centerpiece of U.S. foreign policy. However, as the policy states, properly conceived and well-executed peace operations can be a useful element in serving American interests." (The White

House, PDD-25, May 6 1994) In other words, American interests supersede any humanitarian considerations.

In PDD-25, the U.S. defined the criteria for participation in peacekeeping not only for itself but also for the entire Security Council. According to PDD-25, a peacekeeping mission must advance American interests, reflect a threat or breach of international peace and security, need American participation for its success, include a clear exit strategy and have acceptable costs. These criteria and many others were sufficiently vague and restrictive so that any particular proposed mission could fail to meet the criteria.

On May 9, 1994, the Secretary General proposed a new peacekeeping mission, to be named UNAMIR II, which would expand the existing force of 270 to approximately 5000.

For two weeks, Albright prolonged the debate in order to prevent a new peacekeeping mission from being deployed in Rwanda. In a note from the Office of the Secretary of State to Albright, she is instructed to "Urge the UN to explore and refine this alternative [proposal for UNAMIR II] and present the Council with a menu of at least two options ...along with cost estimates before the Security Council votes on changing UNAMIR's mandate." UNAMIR II passed on May 17, 1994, with a Chapter VII mandate and 5,500 troops. Chicanery would delay the deployment of UNAMIR II until the genocide was over.

The most pernicious delaying tactic involved the need to acquire equipment for deployment of troops in Rwanda and for rescuing trapped civilians. Few countries had the vehicles to perform a rapid airlift and logistics operation needed for the above objectives. American armored personnel carriers (APCs) were available to perform this task enabling the U.S. to engage in further stonewalling. Clinton committed to sending 50 APC's but raised the original estimated cost of the vehicles and demanded that the UN pay for their return. On May 13, 1994, Deputy Secretary of State, Strobe Talbot advised Albright that, "The U.S. is not prepared at this point to lift heavy equipment and troops into Kigali."

On May 17, 1994, when most of the Tutsis and moderate Hutus were dead, the U.S. finally agreed to a modified version of UNAMIR II. Despite the agreement, the Pentagon proceeded in the most tortuously slow manner on the basis of the exact terms of the lease of APC's. By the end of the genocide on July 17, 1994, not one APC had yet arrived in Rwanda.

The case against former President Bill Clinton is very solid given that it clearly meets the requirements of both the Genocide Convention and subsequent court rulings. He knew about the genocide and the intentions of the perpetrators, was extremely diligent in preventing peacekeepers from operating in Rwanda, did violate Article 1 in the Convention, and thereby offered encouragement to the extreme Hutus and prevented a UN force which, according to a number of experts, would have ended the killing. Notwithstanding the strength of the case, it is very unique in the sense that complicity normally requires some kind of direct involvement. Nonetheless, if the UN Security Council was reluctant to act, then U.S. obstruction would not have resulted in a failure to prevent the genocide. Since the Security Council only removed UNAMIR1 due to American pressure and also delayed the deployment of UNAMIR2, then the U.S. actively impeded the Council from preventing or stopping the genocide and at the same time, gave encouragement to the extreme Hutus.

Clinton and the senior officials in his administration are relegated along with G. W. Bush and other Presidents to the ignominious, shameful niche reserved for the reprobates in history whose evil deeds diminish progress towards universal social justice.

By supporting Kagame and Museveni, the U.S. government is responsible for atrocities perpetrated by these brutal dictators. Kagame and Museveni were surrogates for the United States while it was seeking to expand its control over central Africa and purloin valuable resources.

CHAPTER 6

Nigeria

There were a number of hindrances to Nigeria's development. Tribal differences have been a major source of instability but, paradoxically, the abundance of oil in the Niger Delta became a formidable obstacle to any real development. It resulted in the destruction of the traditional way of life of tribes in the Niger Delta and the infringement of their human rights.

Instability was due to three large ethnic groups, each living in a different region of the country and each with its own political party rendering Nigeria almost ungovernable as each group rivaled the other for political power and wealth. The northern part of the country has been dominated by the Hausa-Fulani who were Muslim and believed in feudalism. The West, including the capital, Lagos, was dominated by the Yoruba who were more educated than the Hausa-Fulani and were the most influenced by the West but disdained democracy by dividing their territory into regions ruled by kings. In the East, the most densely populated area, the Ibo eschewed any centrally organized political system and lived in autonomous village societies. They were the most educated of the three groups.

To make matters more difficult, many smaller ethnic groups sought a voice in government and their share of the country's wealth. The Ogoni people numbering 500,000, and Ijaw people, numbering 14 million inhabited the Niger Delta where most of the oil was situated and these tribes became the victims of horrendous human rights violations when foreign oil companies appropriated their land.

Shell British Petroleum, now known as Royal Dutch Shell, was granted permission by the British to explore for oil in 1938. By 1956, Shell had discovered oil in the Niger Delta, immediately setting up operations to extract oil so that by 1958, it was able to export the first barrels of oil from the delta. Mobil Oil Corporation began operations in Nigeria in 1955, Texaco (now part of Chevron) started operations in 1961 and Phillips petroleum (now part of ConocoPhillips) in 1965. By 1979, Nigeria was the sixth largest oil producer in the world, earning $24 billion a year.

Before the discovery of oil, Nigeria was a major leading exporter of groundnuts, cocoa, palm oil, timber, rubber and cashews. Before oil destroyed their ecosystem, sixty percent of the people of the delta were subsistence farmers who flourished on the land and water there.

Unfortunately, the Ogoni people had no voice when the British opened their land to oil exploration and after independence in 1960, they were ignored by the three major ethnic groups. They possessed all the power in Nigeria and benefitted from the wealth flowing from the abundance of oil.

Nigeria became so increasingly dependent on oil exports that by 2008, oil revenues accounted for 97.5% of export revenues, 81% of government revenues and 42% of the GDP. Currently, there are more than 6000 wells in 606 oil fields where oil is then pumped through 7000 kilometers of pipelines, 275 flow stations, 10 gas plants, 4 refineries and 14 export terminals. By 2012, Nigeria produced 2.7 million barrels of oil per day.

As Nigeria was becoming a major producer, it joined the Organization of Petroleum Exporting Companies (OPEC) in 1971 and created the Nigerian National Petroleum Company (NNPC) in 1977. NNPC manages joint ventures between the Nigerian federal government and a number of foreign multinationals including Royal Dutch Shell, ExxonMobil and Chevron.

Devastation of the Niger Delta resulting from the production of oil was a result of collusion between the oil companies working with the Nigerian government and American government support for the leadership in Nigeria, in particular, Olusegan Obasanjo, who ruled from 1976 to 1979 and from 1999 to 2007. Instability was due to frequent changes in leadership because of the three major tribes in Nigeria who fought each other for leadership of the country. These leaders demonstrated a complete lack of interest in the fate of the Ogoni and Ijaw people by refusing to allocate any of the oil wealth to reconstruct or repair the damage caused by the oil companies. Nigeria's government acquired oil money through its joint ventures with the various oil companies through the NNPC and, in return, supported the oil companies in their efforts to remove the inhabitants of the Delta by force, in order to clear the way for oil production and suppress opposition to their operations.

As a result of oil production, the Ogoni and Ijaw people were either killed or lost their means of survival due to the destruction of their environment. When the Ogoni people protested the violation of their rights and destruction of their environment, the Nigerian government cracked down mercilessly to ensure the continuous flow of money from oil production on Ogoni land. According to the World Bank, by 1991, Nigeria was ranked as the thirteenth poorest country in the world despite the tremendous oil wealth in the Niger Delta. Ken Saro-Wiwa, leader of one of the protest groups in the Delta, maintained that the environment in the Ogoni has been:

> Completely devastated by three decades of reckless oil exploitation or ecological warfare by Shell...An ecological warfare is highly lethal...It is homicidal in effect. Human life, flora, fauna, the air, fall at its feet, and finally, the land itself dies.

(Human Rights Watch, *The Price of Oil*, January 1999)

A study by the UN Environmental Programme reported that 1000 square kilometers of Ogoniland was systematically contaminated by Shell Oil. Heavy oil contamination resulted in heavy degradation of water courses even as long as 40 years after a spill. The spills polluted their drinking water with dangerous levels of benzene and hydrocarbons, 1,000 times the level allowed by Nigerian drinking standards. Ravaging of water resources poisoned the fish which was a major staple of the Niger Delta's people's diet. An investigation by Essential Action and Global Exchange reported that:

> Due to the many forms of oil-generated environmental pollution evident throughout the region, farming and fishing have become impossible or extremely difficult in oil-affected areas, and even drinking water has become scarce. Malnourishment

and disease appear common. (Anup Shah, *Nigeria and Oil*, Global Issues, June 10 2010)

Also, UNDP reports that there were more than 6,000 oil spills between 1976 and 2001. Between 1976 and 1991, the oil spills averaged 700 barrels each and the response by the oil companies was slow and damaging. One of the spills at Ebubu in 1970 was set on fire causing irreparable damage to the soil. The National Oil Spill Detection and Response Agency has found that over 2,000 sites have been contaminated by oil spills.

Nigeria's largest spill occurred in January 1980 when 200,000 barrels of oil spilt into the Atlantic Ocean from a Texaco facility destroying 340 hectares of mangroves where it was reported that 180 people died in one community as a result of the spill. In January, 1998, there two major spills. One spill leaked from a Mobil pipeline discharging 40,000 barrels of crude oil onto the Delta while the other dumped 20,000 barrels into a mangrove forest killing an enormous number of fish. Shell attributed the spill to a pipeline failure.

Gas flares were also a major problem burning 24 hours a day, sometimes over a period of 30 years. People in the Ogoni region suffered from the constant noise from the flares and their air was permeated with black soot, contaminating water supplies and causing respiratory problems. As a result of pollution in the Delta, life expectancy for people living there was less than 50 years.

It was not only the spills and flares the inflicted so much damage on the communities in the Delta but, additionally, the infrastructure needed to build and operate the oil facilities. The result of the oil companies constructing roads and dredging canals were dead trees and destroyed fish ponds thereby depriving local communities of the means to sustain themselves.

Niger Delta's importance is global in nature since it is considered to be one of the world's 10 most important wetlands and coastal marine ecosystems. (Amnesty International, *Oil industry has brought poverty and pollution to Niger Delta*, June 30, 2009) According to Amnesty International:

> The United Nation's Development Programme (UNDP) describes the region as suffering from 'administrative' neglect, crumbling social infrastructure and services, high unemployment, social deprivation, abject poverty, filth and squalor, and endemic conflict. (ibid)

Tragically, after the inception of oil production in Nigeria, the ethnic groups living in the Delta went from self-sufficiency to abject poverty and adversity. GNP per capita in the Delta dropped well below the national average of U.S.$260 and unemployment in some regions has been as high as 30%. Attendance at primary schools dropped to less than a third and illiteracy rose sharply. Only 20% to 25% of people in rural communities had access to safe drinking water while proper sanitation was available to less than 25% of the population. State programs of immunization to children had dropped drastically from 85% to 15% between 1989 and 1991.

Reacting to the oil company's violation of their rights in the Delta people who had suffered the ill-effects began forming groups to protest the destruction without compensation by the oil companies and to protest the government's support for these companies.

In the 1990s, Shell strongly supported extensive military attacks against communities and protestors in the Ogoni region by providing military or police units with weapons and ammunition. A letter from the Inspector-General of the Nigerian Police Force to the Managing Director of Shell, dated August 18/94 states that:

> Kindly refer to this office letter...of July 27, 1994, in which approval was given for your company to import some arms and ammunition for the use of the police force to enhance the security of your oil installations.

According to the Centre for Constitutional Rights and EarthRights International:

> At the request of Shell and with Shell's assistance and financing, Nigerian soldiers use deadly force and massive, brutal raids against the Ogoni people throughout the early 1990s to repress a growing movement against the company. (The Centre for Constitutional Rights and Earth Rights International, *The Case Against Shell, April 10 2009*)

Protests began with random attacks in the 1970s and 1980s but organizations began to emerge in the 1990s, the most important of which was the Movement for the Survival of the Ogoni People (MOSOP), founded in 1990 and led by Ken Saro-Wiwa.

In 1990, MOSOP drafted an "Ogoni Bill of Rights" demanding that the Ogoni people have control over their own territory and participate in the government as an autonomous region and that they receive their fair share of oil revenue. It also accused Shell of committing genocide of the Ogoni people. On receiving the "Bill of rights", General Babangida, the head of state, refused to respond.

At the beginning of the U.N.'s International Year of the World's Indigenous People, hundreds of thousands of Ogoni people held a mass rally. Shell withdrew its staff from Ogoni territory charging MOSOP with intimidation of its staff.

Ogoni protests provoked the Nigerian government to undertake a major crackdown of MOSOP leaders during which Ken Saro-Wiwa and other Ogoni leaders were detained several times during 1993. April of that year, the Ogoni people were victims of the first use of military force to suppress a protest of 10,000 people against the construction of a pipeline by the American firm Willbros acting on behalf of Shell. Ten people were wounded.

Also in 1993, a civil war broke out over who would take power in Lagos. Protests erupted demanding a return to democracy inciting brutal government attacks on Ogoni villages leaving 750 people dead and 30,000 homeless. Homes and property were destroyed.

To further quell any uprising, the government formed a military unit in 1994 known as the River State Internal Security Task Force. Human rights abuses conducted by the Task Force included detentions, harassment and extrajudicial executions of Ogoni activists. Sixteen members of the MOSOP leadership were arrested and convicted, nine of whom were sentenced to death including Saro-Wiwa by a special tribunal which ignored due process. The State refused to present any evidence against Saro-Wiwa. The nine were executed on November 10, 1995. The Centre for Constitutional Rights claims that: "The detention, trial, and executions of the Ogoni Nine were the result of collusion between Shell and the military government to suppress opposition to Shell's oil production in Nigeria."

According to Human Rights Watch who visited the Ogoni people and spoke to eye witnesses about cases in which:

> Individuals marked as MOSOP activists had been extrajudicially executed, beaten, or detained by members of the security forces. In raids by the security forces on houses where such activists live, police or soldiers often assaulted all members of the household indiscriminately. (Bronwen Manby, *The Price of Oil*, Human Rights Watch, January 1999)

Both the oil companies and Washington supported attempts by the Nigerian government to suppress any uprising or protests against both the oil companies who were destroying their way of life and against the Nigerian government who refused to protect or compensate them for any loss of life or damage caused by oil production.

One of the mechanisms employed by Washington to support oil production in the Delta was its failure to regulate the actions of its multinationals operating outside the country and also its failure to support any legal claims by the victims of oil company's negligent, reckless and criminal behaviour.

For example, in a case before the U.S. Supreme Court in early 2012, Kiobel v. Royal Dutch Petroleum Co. (Shell), the relatives of the nine Ogoni activists, including Ken Saro-Wiwa, charged that the military dictatorship in Nigeria allegedly worked in collaboration with Shell.

They claim that over a ten year period, they have been trying to prove in court that the British-Dutch multinational company conspired with the Nigerian military to illegally detain, torture and kill critics of Shells illegal and immoral practises in the Niger Delta.

The Obama administration submitted a brief arguing that the U.S. Supreme Court did not have jurisdiction in this case despite an 18th century law, Alien Torts Claims (ATCA), that has authorized U.S. courts to hear cases where plaintiffs bring international violations cases to U.S. federal courts.

Shell paid out $383 million to the Nigerian military and private firms between 2007 and 2009 to secure its oil facilities from attack or protests by local inhabitants. In 2009 alone, it gave $65 million to Nigerian military forces and $75 million for other security costs consisting mostly of private security firms. Additionally, Shell supplied government forces with gunboats, helicopters, vehicles and cell phones. Large-scale military attacks were carried out by the government in 2009 which resulted in the displacement of tens of thousands of residents.

Heavily armed soldiers violated the human rights in the Ogoni village of Kaa where 35 civilians were killed. Not only did Shell supply helicopters and arms to the Nigerian soldiers but Lieutenant-Colonel Paul Okuntimo was paid by Shell and driven around the Delta in a Shell vehicle.

As well, Shell facilities were guarded by a large network of Mobile Police (MOPOL), the joint task force, a combination of the army, navy and police and a 1,200 strong internal police force.

Chevron's oil operations in the Delta resulted in similar destruction of the environment and human rights violations. To protect its facilities, Chevron also made helicopters available to Nigerian troops provoking 200 demonstrators to take control of a Chevron oil platform for three days. The manager of the platform called in Nigerian troops who were transported in Chevron helicopters. Two demonstrators were killed and two months later, four more were killed in a similar incident. Sixty-seven people were missing after Nigerian forces attacked two small villages using Chevron helicopters and boats.

Alliance between the Nigerian government and Shell was confirmed in a U.S. court on June 8, 2008, where the Ogoni people had launched a lawsuit against Shell, charging them with collusion with the government in crimes against humanity and gross human rights abuses. (John Vidal, *Shell Oil paid Nigerian Military to put down protests, court documents show*, The Guardian, October 3 20011) Shell was forced to pay out $15.5 million in damages.

Additionally, Washington supported Nigeria militarily, notably, when Olusegan Obasanjo was president despite his human right's record while protecting the oil companies from protests or attacks.

The United States provided $1.5 million in training grants to the Nigerian military from 1962 to 1972. Then, between 1972 and 1990, $63 million in defense articles and services were delivered to Nigeria. Since 1986, funding for military training and education amounted to $90,000 per year.

In his final state of the Union Address, President Carter framed the "Carter Doctrine" which declared that the U.S. would use "any means necessary, including military force" to protect its oil supply which was defined as a "vital interest". It was extended to West Africa, in particular, Nigeria, in 2002 when Assistant Secretary of State, Walter Kansteiner stated that: "African oil is a strategic national interest to us...[and] it will increase and become more important as we move forward." (Mike Crawly, *With Mideast uncertainty, US turns to Africa for oil*, Christian Science Monitor, May 23 2002)

President Clinton created the African Crisis Response Initiative (ACRI) to expand the American security framework to Africa involving more military activities on the continent and more military assistance. In 2004, ACRI was renamed African Contingency Operations Training and Assistance Program (ACOTA) broadening the scope of the program and specifically targeting Nigeria with more military assistance to protect America's supply of oil.

Clinton also negotiated a military pact with Nigeria called the Nigeria and US Military Pact which called for a private company to perform the following functions:

1. to implement a plan to install civilian control over the military;
2. to redefine the military's three branches;
3. to trim the bloated forces;
4. to devise a strategy for dealing with officers who lost their jobs.

During a visit to Nigeria in the spring of 2000, Defense Secretary William S. Cohen announced a $10.6 million military aid package and remarked that: "We want to have a long and enduring relationship with Nigeria because we recognize that Nigeria is going to be a very important country in terms of its role throughout Africa." (Douglas Farah, *U.S. to Help Nigeria Revamp Its Armed Forces*, Washington Post, April 29 2000, A14)

The Bush Administration recognized the potential to secure an increasing oil supply from West Africa where Nigeria would be the main producer. Dick Cheney chaired the National Energy Policy Development Group (NEPDG) which issued the Report of the National Energy Policy Development Group on May 17, 2001. In the report, it is noted that: "West Africa is expected to be one of the fastest-growing sources of oil and natural gas for the American market...giving it a growing market share for refining centers on the East Coast of the United States." Moreover, it states that: "The U.S. Agency for International Development has provided technical assistance in support of West Africa...and is providing assistance for the creation of a regulatory framework that will enable Ghana and Nigeria to become major exporters of natural gas and electricity." (National Energy Policy Development Group, *Reliable, Affordable and Environmentally Sound Energy for America's Future*, May 17 2001)

Cheney's report did not refer at all to the human rights atrocities perpetrated by the oil companies in the Niger delta but only focused on West Africa exclusively as a means to diversify American oil supply.

On July 9, 2003, President George W. Bush paid a visit to Nigeria to meet with Obasanjo in order to persuade him to opt out of OPEC to ensure that Nigeria would not be subject to OPEC's influence. As well, Bush applied pressure on Obasanjo to adopt neoliberal economic policies by promoting privatization and removal of subsidies. These policies would further impoverish the people of Nigeria.

To reduce America's dependence on unstable supplies from the Middle East and to promote diversification of sources of oil, West Africa would minimize the problem of "Concentration of world oil production in any one region of the world."

Reaffirming the importance of West African oil, Donald R. Norland, former U.S. ambassador to Chad, reported to the African Subcommittee of the U.S. House International Relations Committee, that: "Africa and national security - have been used in the same sentence in Pentagon documents." (Donald R. Norland, *Subcommittee on Africa Hearing*, House of Representatives, Serial No. 107-75, April 18 2002)

In 2006, the Congressional Budget Justification for Foreign Operations notes Nigeria's: "importance as a leading supplier of petroleum to the U.S." and "disruption of supply from Nigeria would represent a major blow to the oil security of the U.S."

When Obama took office, he accepted the policies of the NEPDG and became determined to expand the use of military force in Africa. Reviewing the budget requests submitted by the State Department and Defense Department for Nigeria in 2010 reveal the extent to which Obama is committed to a strong military involvement. For example:

1. State Department (arms sales, military training) – $1.4 million;
2. International Military Education and Training - $1.1 million;

3. Narcotics Control and Law Enforcement - $2 million;
4. Anti-terrorism Assistance Program - $228 million (all sub-Saharan counties);
5. Defense Department (counter-terrorism, AFRICOM) - $278 million.

During Hillary Clinton's visit to Nigeria, she reassured the Foreign Minister and Defense Minister that:

> [She] had some very specific suggestions as to how the United States could assist the Nigerian government in their efforts to try to bring peace and stability to the Niger Delta. We have a very good relationship between our two militaries. So I will be talking with my counterpart, the Secretary of Defense, and we will through our joint efforts...determine what Nigeria would want from us for help.

(African Security Research Project, *U.S. Military Involvement in Nigeria*, September 2009)

In the event that a conflict flares up in the Delta between the protesters and the government, Washington planned to intervene to maintain order and security. Pentagon planners have been preparing for a direct military intervention in the Delta given a potential disruption of oil production or delivery.

Securing a steady oil supply from Nigeria also meant maintaining leaders in power who could be trusted. One of those leaders was Obasanjo.

Obasanjo captured the presidency after the assassination of Murtala Muhammad in 1976. American leaders were worried by Muhammad's pan-African proclivities and their concern that they could not depend on him to supply oil, particularly if another oil crisis erupted whereas Obasanjo had established close ties to the CIA and Washington. The ultimate affront to Washington occurred when Muhammad declined an offer by Henry Kissinger to pay an official visit to Nigeria in May of 1976 to reassure the American government that Nigeria could be counted on to supply oil in the event of another oil crisis.

One month after Muhammad took office, a feasibility study prepared by the Pentagon in August 21, 1975, "Oil Fields as Military Objectives", was presented to Congress which examined the option for a military invasion of the Nigerian coast if American vital oil interests were threatened.

There is strong evidence showing that the CIA was responsible for the assassination of Muhammad. According to the U.S. Information Agency's (USIS) country plan for Nigeria: "Charges of U.S. (CIA) backing for the attempted coup were prevalent." (U.S. Information Service, *Country Plan for Nigeria*, 1976)

Obasanjo had developed close relationships with key persons and agencies in the U.S. He had been friends with Donald B. Easum who was the American ambassador to Nigeria at the time of the assassination of Muhammad.

He gave a lecture at the Centre for Strategic and International Studies (CSIS), where Henry Kissinger served as counsellor and from which Obasanjo launched the African leadership Forum to which Robert McNamara had connections. Additionally, he hosted a meeting of religion and politics at the US Institute of Peace, which was U.S.-government controlled. As well, Obasanjo was appointed to the Board of the African American Institute which had been set up with CIA money.

Obasanjo's connections to the American government and the CIA explain his overriding concern about the uninterrupted flow of oil to the United States despite the human rights atrocities of the oil companies. He turned a blind eye to the plight of his own people in the Niger Delta so that oil companies could operate unimpeded by legal and human rights considerations.

President Goodluck Jonathan has been the head of Nigeria since his succession in 2010, selected according to the constitutional provision for replacement of President who dies in office. The previous president had been Umaru Yar'adua. Jonathan was re-elected in 2011.

Jonathan inherited a country wracked by poverty, instability, conflict and a populace deeply embittered and enraged at the horrors inflicted on them by foreign oil companies, Western interference and corrupt and brutal leaders.

To assuage the restless population, he promised to eradicate violent groups and to implement a progressive program to improve the lives of Nigerians. His proposal, the Transformation Agenda, was a five year plan to promote non-inflationary growth, job creation and poverty alleviation.

Implementation of his agenda was only moderately successful and according to the Journal of Research and Development, "The effect was not significant enough to overcome the challenges of poverty, unemployment, security and industrialization." (Oladimeh, D. and Opeyemi, I. Journal of Research and Development: Vol. 1, No. 1, 2013)

In addition, Jonathan was extremely ineffective in quelling outbreaks of violence by groups opposed to the government. Resorting to brutal tactics only emboldened these groups, some of who sought to establish a Muslim government with Sharia law.

One very violent group with ties to al Qaeda, Boko Haram, who kidnapped 276 girls in mid-April 2014, has a polymorphously diverse history. Its origins sprang from the social and economic conditions in Nigeria resulting to a large extent from exploitation by Western oil companies in collaboration with the federal government in Nigeria. Once the group existed in inchoate form, al Qaeda moved in to capitalize on the strong anti-Western, fundamentalist Islamic character of the group to mobilize it for its own purposes.

To gain a comprehensive understanding of Boko Haram necessitates an examination of its colonial past under British rule. Britain drew the boundaries for Nigeria in 1903 partly by the victory in the North over the Bornu Empire consisting of Hausa Kingdoms, one of the largest ethnic groups in Africa, and the Sokoto Caliphate.

The people in the North resented western evangelism and losing control over their land and culture. Ultimately the Hausa strongly rejected western ideals and education and resented the preference of the British towards the Christian South where they built schools and infrastructure.

After Nigeria gained its independence in 1960, the people of the North frequently rebelled against both a corrupt government and Western values. This resentment manifested itself in a hatred of Western education which is the primary founding principle of Boko Haram.

One of the men who had a significant impact on the Muslims in the North, and in particular, the youth, was the cleric known as Maitatsine whose words resonated with the poor and marginalized youth.

In the late 1990s, Mohammed Yusuf became the leader of this movement and in 2002 he founded Boko Haram with the intention of converting the youth to his brand of Islam. He established a religious complex comprising a school and a mosque which attracted people from all of Nigeria.

Boko Haram turned violent and launched military campaigns in 2009 to create an Islamic state. Since their militarization, the group has killed about 4,000 people and has attacked police stations, government buildings and schools.

Poverty in Nigeria has motivated many young people to join Boko haram. Despite recent reports that Nigeria's economy has soared to new heights, it still remains one of the poorest countries on the planet where 68% of workers earn less than $1.25 a day and 84% of workers earn less than $2.00 a day. Fallacies in the GDP measurement account for this discrepancy which can easily be explained by the huge gap in the distribution of wealth. As well, there is a wide gap between the wealth in the North which is mostly Muslim and the wealth in the south with is mostly Christian.

Poverty encompasses many other problems. "Nigeria has one of the highest rates of infant mortality in the world. One in seven children dies before their fifth birthday. The United Nations (UN) Standing Committee on Nutrition asserts that malnutrition is the largest contributor to non-communicable diseases in the world. Nigeria is believed to be home to 10 million of such children (stunting due to malnutrition." (Akintade, K. *13% of Nigerian children malnourished.* Daily Times, September 13, 2012)

Nigeria ranks tenth in oil reserves in the world which could have raised the standard of living substantially for Nigerians had Western oil companies not looted $140 billion a year in oil revenues from Nigerian reserves while Nigeria receives a paltry 9% royalty.

To exacerbate the problem, the IMF insisted as one of its conditionalities that Nigeria drop its oil subsidy increasing the price of oil by 120%. The rise in prices triggered a national strike among trade unionists forcing Jonathan to partly back down.

In addition, the IMF required the Nigerian government to sell Nigeria's oil refineries which forced the government to import refined oil. According to the Bretton Wood's Project, "It is estimated that the federal government spent a total of $18.6 billion from 2000-2006 to import refined petroleum products." (Baker, L. *Facilitating Whose Power?* Bretton Woods Project, April 2, 2008)

The critical issue is the extent to which Western oil companies robbed Nigerians of oil revenue that belonged to them. In 2013, Chevron alone averaged 233,000 barrels a day in Nigeria. At the same time, two-thirds of the people of Nigeria garner their energy needs from burning fuel wood and agricultural wastes. It is sadly ironic that the nation with the tenth largest reserves of oil still relies on such a primitive means to generate energy. Sixty percent of the population lacks access to electricity.

Suffering of this magnitude is bound to produce disgruntled, resentful and angry citizens who would be quick to lash out at the causes of their ill-fate which includes their own government, foreign oil companies, foreign governments who support them and the elites or dominant groups in their own country.

Nigeria is clearly another example of a major power using a foreign government as a proxy to maintain order by squelching protests against the major power's multi-national corporations who were literally stealing a valuable resource. This theft denied Nigerian people resources that were necessary for their own development and at the same time, resulted in the loss of their lives and means of survival.

CHAPTER 7

Liberia/Sierra Leone

Liberia is an exceptional case among African countries. It was founded by approximately 300 ex-slaves from the United States who formed the first independent Nation on the continent in 1847.

Black settlers were originally slaves from the United States who were benefactors of a movement called the American Colonization Society who advocated for returning slaves to their place of origin. Former slaves became the new elite in a territory eventually known as Liberia.

From 1877 to 1980, the country was ruled by a single party whose members came from the new elite, the ex-slaves. The American-Liberians constructed a colonial system which relegated the indigenous population to the status of second-class citizens.

American exploitation of Liberia had its roots in the conjunction of growth in the rubber industry and demand for automobiles. The State Department sought a concession from the Liberian government to open up rubber resources for the Firestone Tire and Rubber Company whereby Firestone offered the Liberian government a $5 million loan in exchange for one million acres of rubber trees at six cents an acre for 99 years.

The Liberian government was supplying slave labour to the Firestone plantation as well as to Spanish controlled plantations. To investigate the violations of workers' rights, the League of Nations established a commission, headed by British jurist Cuthbert Christy, to determine the extent of forced labour in Liberia. Christy's report concluded that: "Labour for private purposes is forcibly impressed by the [Liberian] Government and used in the Firestone Plantations." (Dr. Cuthbert Christy, Charles S. A. Johnson & Arthur Barclay, *The Christy-report*, 1930) This corrupt recruitment system supplied labour to Firestone until the early 1960's.

Iron ore, abundant in the Bomi hills, was another Liberian resource desperately needed, especially during World War II. To mine iron ore in the Bomi hills, American steel companies needed a port from which to ship the ore to America. In 1943, America and Liberia signed the Port Agreement both satisfying the need to ship ore to America and realizing Washington's dream of a naval base on the west coast of Africa.

Finally in 1945, a mining concession was granted for development of iron ore mines in the Bomi Hills which extended to American mining companies exclusive mining rights for an eighty year period covering three million acres. A royalty of only five cents per ton was to be paid to the Liberian government for every ton of ore that was mined. In addition, the mining companies were exempt from paying any taxes on the ore which was exported back to the United States.

Despite the exploitation, the Liberian government earned revenues from these industries. In addition, registration of ships became a burgeoning source of revenue given the government's low standards and lack of inspection.

These three sources of income constituted 50 per cent of government revenues although most of it flowed to the rich elite exacerbating a growing disparity between the elites and the majority of the impoverished tribal population. This disparity subsequently led to protests for a more equitable distribution of wealth. Martin Meredith described the inequality of wealth as: "The Americo-Liberians constructed a colonial system subjugating the indigenous population to rigid control and concentrating wealth and privilege in their own hands." (Martin Meredith, *The Fate of Africa: A History of Fifty Years of Independence*, 2005, p. 544)

Early exploitation in Liberia was based on stealing resources, cheap labor and low taxes for American multinationals and maintaining friendly dictators in power thus depriving the Liberian people of access to the resources they could have utilized to advance their own economic development.

During and after World War II, Liberia became a useful and convenient ally in America's efforts to defeat the Axis powers and to halt the expansion of communism. To instil fear in the U.S. population, the threat of an international subversive communist movement bent on global expansion was propagated to conceal the real America agenda which was to gain control over the so-called 'Grand Area' and to justify enormous defence expenditures.

During World War II, the United States initiated its plan to use Liberia as a strategic base for its anti-communist agenda by signing a defence pact with Liberia calling for the construction of roads, airports and other infrastructure projects. A key element of this plan was the building of Robertsfield Airport with runways sufficiently long for B-47 bombers to land and refuel.

To accommodate increased diplomatic and intelligence traffic between the U.S. and Liberia and to monitor broadcasts in the region, the CIA built the largest spy station in all of Africa that provided communications for 34 Embassies and Consulates.

When William Tubman became president in 1944, there was an agreement to offer the U.S. free land in exchange for aid. In order to undermine national liberation movements in Africa during the Cold War, the U.S. invested billions of dollars in intelligence equipment in Liberia. As well, Liberia became an outpost to relay voice of America broadcasts throughout the region.

To guide shipping traffic in the eastern Atlantic and along the west coast of Africa, the American Coast Guard built an omega navigational station in Paynesville, a suburb of Monrovia, the capital of Liberia. In addition, Washington acquired the right to establish military installations in the Monrovia port in the event that: "They become necessary for the maintenance of international peace and security." (Memorandum from U.S. Embassy to Secretary of State, 1979)

Clearly, the purpose of these military installations and facilities were to further the American agenda of defeating communist incursions and furthering American imperial objectives in Africa. Naval ports, surveillance equipment and runways to accommodate American bombers can only be intended for imperialistic objectives. According to the Journal of Pan African Studies:

> During World War II, the United States continued the process of transferring Liberia into a neo-colony...Thereafter (beginning in 1945 to 1989), the U.S. took other steps, including the support for various authoritarian regimes, the continual use of Liberia to advance American strategic interests...
>
> (George Klay Keih, Jr., *Neo-Colonialism: American Foreign Policy and the First Liberian War*, Pan African Studies, Vol. 5, March 2012)

Furthermore, Noah Leavitt describes America's foreign policy toward Liberia: "[A] special relationship is based on using Liberia's resources to advance its security interests, and for economic gain." (Noah Leavitt, *One Big Prison Yard, Counterpunch*, April 12-14)

Liberia was ruled by William Tubman from 1944 to 1971, and William Tolbert from 1871 to 1980. Both leaders maintained close ties to the United States and were rewarded with $500 million in military and economic aid from 1946 to 1960 and $280 million from 1962 to 1980.

Both were committed to supporting the American objectives of containing communism in Africa. In terms of advancing America's economic interests, Tubman was more supportive of the current agreements while Tolbert sought to redress the loss of revenue from the exploitation of resources.

Tubman was the more U.S.-friendly of the two engendering the expectation on the part of Americans that, according to Liberian expert Elwood Dunn:

> US engagement with the Liberian regime was predicated on the expectation that Liberia would play a surrogate role in the sub-region and beyond, would support the U.S. Policy of containing the spread of communism, and would probably address the concerns of US missionary and business interests in the country. (D. Elwood Dunn, *Liberia and the United States During the Cold war: Limits of Reciprocity,* September 2009)

Tubman travelled extensively to gain support for foreign investment in mining the newly discovered mineral deposits. He built roads, schools and hospitals and expanded the right to vote but during his time in office, the gap between the elites and indigenous people widened.

Nearing the end of his rule, he gravitated toward a more authoritarian regime, changing the constitution to secure another term in office and clamping down on dissent in the media and on members of the opposition as popular opposition to his rule grew.

In 1971, William Tolbert assumed the office of the presidency. Whereas Tubman's international travels abroad were intended to search for new investors, Tolbert's excursions were intended to expand Liberia's ties to the rest of the world. Notwithstanding his intention to retain strong ties to the United States, he also established ties with the Soviet Union and Romania. In addition, he courted favor with China and Cuba by inviting their ambassadors to Liberia. Given the fact that the U.S. was counting heavily on Liberia as a bulwark against a communist incursion into Africa, these new relations deeply troubled Washington.

As well, Tolbert's pan-African posturing was another impediment to America's strategy in Africa. A united Africa was anathema to America's intention to exploit individual countries both economically and strategically.

Tolbert embarked on a policy of reform by increasing freedoms and dismantling the patronage networks but the great disparity between the elites and the indigenous population widened.

When Tolbert spent half the national budget hosting an Organization of African Unity (OAU) conference while at the same time, rice, the staple food of Liberians, doubled in price, protestors took to the streets. Tolbert ordered the police and army to open fire on protestors many of whom were killed in the onslaught.

Charges of treason and sedition were filed against opposition members who had called for a general strike and their party was banned. With the rising tide of opposition to his presidency, it was not surprising when a 28-year old master-sergeant, Samuel Doe, successfully perpetrated a bloody coup against Tolbert on April 12, 1980. The coup resulted in the murder of 200 people and 500 political opponents were thrown into prison.

Doe was a 28-year-old master sergeant, trained in the United States, whose tribe, the Krahn, were small in number and considered to be the least educated of all the tribes in Liberia. During the course of the next ten years, he appointed his fellow tribesman to all the powerful positions in the government and the military.

On taking power, Doe announced a number of progressive measures which he promised to implement such as restoring civilian power, liberating the masses from corruption and oppression and establishing a more equitable distribution of wealth.

Instead of fulfilling those promises he became a corrupt and brutal dictator whose conduct first lost him the support of the U.S. Congress and eventually, President W. H. Bush turned his back on him.

He created the People's Redemption Council of which he was the chairman with 17 soldiers as its members. His first action as Chair of the Council was to suspend the constitution following which he ruled as a dictator until he was overthrown in a coup in 1990.

Opposition to his rule was prohibited, resulting in imprisonment for student leaders, journalists and opposition members who criticized his regime. Newspapers were shut down and academics were flogged for any activities that cast aspersions on his regime.

Doe and his fellow tribesman amassed a fortune estimated to be $300 million by looting state corporations such as the Liberian Petroleum Refining Corporation, the Liberian Produce Marketing Corporation and the Forest Development Corporation.

Despite his corruption, brutality and violations of human rights, Doe enjoyed strong support from the United States who were determined to protect their commercial and strategic interests. He was one of many dictators who, notwithstanding their corruption and brutality, were maintained in power to advance and defend American interests. By supporting these dictators, including Doe, the United States condemned the people in these countries to slow or no economic development and dreadful suffering resulting from the dictator's need to suppress any opposition or enemies.

In September 1980, Washington sent Richard M. Moose, Assistant Secretary of State for African Affairs to Liberia to assess Doe's position vis-à-vis the United States and to recommend policies to strengthen ties between the two countries. Two of his recommendations were to "Support military training, provide new equipment to the military, and build enlisted housing" and to "Support long-term development of the country." (William H. McCoy, Jr., *Senegal and Liberia: Case Studies in U.S. IMET Training*, Rand Corporation, March 2012, p.12) U.S. military and economic aid to Liberia between 1981 and 1985 was $402 million.

Throughout the next ten years, the *Department of State Congressional Presentations for Security Assistance Programs* defined the purpose of aid to Liberia as necessary to "Enhance cooperative defense and security".

In fact, these ambiguous policies translated into securing the surveillance, intelligence, communications and navigational facilities on which the United States relied in its struggle against communism.

Reagan's National Security Decision Directive 101 (NSDD) on September 2, 1983 stipulated that: "Liberia is important to the United states as the site of a variety of valuable U.S. facilities, military access rights, and private investment." (President Reagan, *U.S. Strategy Towards Liberia, National Security Decision Directives*, NSC-NSDD-101, September 1983)

In the same directive, he advised that the U.S. government should: "Step up contact with the army and the People's Redemption Council to improve discipline and professionalism." (ibid) Obviously, democracy and human rights were secondary priorities behind protecting American facilities and strengthening the Liberian army. It was the Peoples Redemption Council that created the authoritarian regime in the first place.

An understanding was reached between Reagan and Doe in which the U.S. would ensure the strength of the Liberian army and provide aid while Doe would take measures to accommodate the U.S. Doe's part of the bargain was to close the Libyan diplomatic mission in Liberia, order reductions in the size of the Soviet mission and establish diplomatic relations with Israel. As well, Doe agreed to a change in the mutual defense pact with an extension to staging rights on 24-hour notice at Liberia's sea and airports for the U.S. Rapid Deployment Force, the purpose of which was to respond to security threats around the world.

In addition, Doe assented to the use of Liberian territory as a staging ground for America's wars against other African nations. These operations were directed at Gaddafi in Libya where the CIA was supporting organized resistance to Gaddafi. In Angola, UNITA was supported by the U.S. with Liberia acting as a staging ground. A covert operation in support of Chadian leader Hissene Habre was also based in Liberia.

Reagan continued his support for Doe throughout the first half of the decade despite the fact that Doe and his ministers were stealing most of the aid money and Doe had suspended any pretense of democracy or respect for human rights.

When Doe stole the 1985 election, there was a backlash in the U.S. Congress where there was reluctance to fund a leader who flouted democratic norms. At the outset, Doe had banned the two most popular opposition parties, arresting its leaders, and then proceeded to make it illegal for any citizen to criticize the government. To further suppress any opposition, he closed the Observer, the most popular independent media in Liberia.

As well, when preliminary votes indicated that Doe was losing the election, his election officials suspended the vote-counting and created a special committee stacked with Doe supporters to recount the ballots. Two weeks later, the recount committee announced that Doe had won the election. According the Lawyers Committee for Human Rights, the election was: "One of the most brazen electoral frauds in recent African History." (Martin Merideth, *The Fate of Africa: History of the Continent Since Independence*, September 6 2011, p. 552)

Since Washington's priorities have been to advance their national interests and not to promote democracy in other countries, the Reagan administration defended the election as a good start. Chester Crocker, Reagan's senior policy-maker on Africa claimed that: "There is now the beginning, however imperfect, of a democratic experience that Liberia and its friends can use as a benchmark." (Charles P. Henry, *Foreign Policy and the Black (Inter)National Interest*, 2000, p.

141) Crocker also referred to Liberia as: "a civilian government based on elections…an ongoing tradition among the citizenry of speaking out, and a new constitution which protects these freedoms." (David Harris, Civil War and Democracy in West Africa, January 15 2012, p. 70) Reagan's attitude toward Doe and his administration contrasted sharply with a disillusioned Congress which immediately joined the rest of the world in condemning the elections and passed a non-binding resolution to suspend military and economic aid to Liberia until confirmation was forthcoming that Doe was moving towards democracy.

Doe arrived at a crossroads in his presidency in 1985 after the naked grab for power in the election when he destroyed any hope for democracy during his rule and the resulting resentment led to a failed coup attempt one month following the elections. The leader of the coup was Thomas Quiwonkpa who came to prominence in the 1980 military coup against Tolbert leading to his ascendancy as head of the Armed Forces of Liberia (AFL). In 1983, he fell out of favor with Doe after which he fled the country.

Crossing into Liberia from Sierra Leone, Quiwonkpa and about 24 heavily armed men marched into Monrovia, seized the military barracks and government radio station in order to broadcast a message calling for free elections. As news of the possible coup disseminated through Monrovia, crowds began to celebrate in the streets in the hope of a successful coup. With the help of some of his army units and a warning from the CIA about the impending coup, Doe regained control, thus dashing any hopes that his presidency was about to end.

The repercussions of the coup were a spate of fiercely brutal acts of revenge inflicted on tribes opposed to his rule, especially Quiwonkpa's Gio tribe. Gio and Mano soldiers and civilians living in Monrovia were rounded up and executed while hundreds more Gios were murdered in Nimba county. Doe's slaughter of about 3,000 people sowed the seeds of an ethnic rivalry which resulted in a civil war five years later.

However, Reagan continued to support Doe during the second half of the 1980's despite his atrocious record on human rights and his neglect of the people in terms of their standard of living and lack of democracy. To exemplify the willful ignorance of conditions in Liberia under Doe's rule, consider the following report from Assistant Secretary of State for African Affairs, Chester Crocker:

> We believe there has been a movement in a positive direction. If you take a moving picture, it shows a trend which we think is a good one. If you take a snapshot, then in the snapshot you can see problems. Problems are not absent, but the situation has improved. (Human Rights Watch, *Liberia: Flight from Terror,* May 1, 1990)

As is frequently the case when an American president supports a dictator, once the dictator proves to be loyal to the extent that he will sacrifice his own country's interests for those of the United States, he will continue to enjoy the President's backing.

In fact, neglect of the economy and social programs were exacting an enormous toll on the Liberian people. In his first five years in power, the economy contracted by 3% a year; domestic investment decreased by 16%; decline in foreign investment; 50% unemployment and foreign debt rose to $1.3 billion. In addition, 80% of the population was illiterate and by the year 2,000, 63% of Liberians lived below the poverty line and 48% lived in extreme poverty.

U.S. aid and investment were primarily targeted at improving Liberian security and American military capabilities. Given the conditions of the Liberian people, maintaining Doe in power was an obstacle to development and to ameliorating the lives of the Liberian people. In addition, exacerbating tribal hatred, after the failed coup attempt, ultimately led to the bitter civil war which opened the door for Charles Taylor's brutal regime.

Charles Taylor was born into an Americo-Liberian family in Arlington, who, upon graduating from high school, was sent to Bentley College in Boston to obtain an economics degree followed by a graduate degree in New Hampshire. In total, he spent nine years in the United States.

Charles Taylor worked as director of the government's procurement agency until he was accused of embezzling and was forced to leave the country. He sought refuge in the United States only to be arrested after an extradition request. Taylor languished in jail while waiting for the outcome of an appeal; then escaped in 1985 and found his way to West Africa.

During the next several years, Taylor travelled around West Africa organizing his own band of supporters. While in Côte d'Ivoire he organized 160 dissidents into an armed group called the National liberation Front of Liberia (NPFL) which was eventually united with members of the Gio and Mano tribes in Liberia who were already rebelling against Doe' regime. Libya, always seeking to undermine pro-American governments, provided some of the funding for the NPFL.

On December 24, 1989, with the assistance of two West-African leaders from Côte d'Ivoire and Burkina Faso, and with dissidents from Sierra Leone, Nigeria, Ghana and Gambia, Taylor marched into Nimba County in Liberia from Côte d'Ivoire. His attempts to gain control of the government led to civil war.

One of the new factions that emerged during the civil war was the result of a split between Taylor and Prince Johnson who formed a splinter rebel group known as the Independent National Patriotic Front of Liberia (INPFL). INPFL forces were as brutal and monstrous as the NPFL and the AFL.

As expected, Doe despatched a Krahn counter-insurgency force to Nimba County to defeat the rebels. On their march towards the rebels, Doe's forces subjected the local populations to a vicious campaign of terror involving killing, raping, looting, burnt villages and driving tens of thousands of Gios and Manos from their homes.

The brutality of Doe's army was a recruiting apparatus for vengeful Gios and Manos who were eager to join forces with Taylor. Many of these recruits were illiterate teenagers and boys who were uncontrollable, undisciplined and psychopathic. These child soldiers, bolstered by various drugs, ravaged the countryside on their march toward Monrovia by killing, raping and pillaging.

Deliberate targeting of civilians by all sides resulted in egregious violations of human rights and humanitarian law. Taylor's and Johnson's forces were attacking the Krahn tribe and Doe's army was attacking members of the Gios and Manos tribe.

Besides the killing, raping and pillaging, these atrocities resulted in massive numbers of internally displaced people and a terror-stricken population who lived in constant fear. As the atrocities escalated, a number of people fled to neighboring countries such as Guinea and Côte d'Ivoire and in total, half the population was estimated to have been displaced by 1990.

By June 1990, Monrovia was under siege from Taylor's forces in the East and Johnson's forces from the West. Intense fighting for control of Monrovia erupted during three battles in 1990, 1992 and 1996. During each battle, more of Monrovia fell to the rebel forces and a greater number of people fell victim to the cruelty of all the warring parties.

In May 1990, Sierra Leone, not unaffected by the war, announced that it was intending to fund peace talks in Freetown, the capital, to be organized by the Economic Community of West African States (ECOWAS) consisting of Ghana, Guinea, Sierra Leone, Gambia, Mali, Burkina Faso and Nigeria.

On August 6, leaders of the Standing Mediation Committee (SMC), a committee of ECOWAS, met in Gambia to resolve the humanitarian crisis in Liberia and agreed to a peace plan calling for an immediate ceasefire to be monitored by a group called Economic Community of West African States (ECOMOG) Monitoring Group, a fighting force created by ECOWAS. ECOWAS was committed to organizing free and fair elections and to stemming the tide of carnage in Liberia.

Overlooking a basic principle of peacekeeping, that all parties must consent to the mission, was the downfall of the ECOWAS initiative since Charles Taylor, a major party in the process was completely opposed to the idea of a peacekeeping mission and threatened to attack ECOMOG forces if they tried to intervene. On September 9, 1990, Prince Johnson and INPFL troops captured Samuel Doe at a meeting brokered by ECOMOG and assassinated him. Doe's assassination called into question the effectiveness of ECOMOG due to the fact that Doe was captured on a visit to their headquarters.

Nevertheless, ECOMOG was able to secure Monrovia followed by the formation of an interim government in which Amos Sawyer, a political scientist, was installed as leader. Taylor rejected the interim government thus rendering it virtually useless in its capacity to govern Liberia. Disagreement over the legitimacy of the interim government led to a number of agreements between ECOWAS and Taylor all of which were broken by Taylor who then, each time, continued his assaults on Monrovia.

Taylor's expansionary aspirations for West Africa involved Sierra Leone with its vast wealth of diamonds. In November, 1990, Taylor threatened to capture Freetown's international airport claiming that it was being used as an operational base for ECOMOG forces. By March 1991, armed Liberian soldiers in Southern Sierra Leone launched attacks on Freeport forces which quickly escalated into a bloody, brutal civil war.

Taylor armed and financed a group of fighters calling themselves the Revolutionary United Front (RUF), led by Foday Sankoh and comprised of Sierra Leone dissidents, hardened NPFL units and mercenaries. On March 23, 1991, 100 members of RUF crossed the border into Sierra Leone and captured several villages. Its primary purpose was to gain control of the diamond fields of Kono for themselves and for Taylor.

Sanko's rebellion was bent on abducting young boys whom they would then convert into rabid, pathological killers. Part of the indoctrination process of these young boys was to first murder their own parents and imbibe a number of drugs, including amphetamines, in order to convert them into psychotic killers. They were encouraged to support themselves by looting and killing. Once involved, it was almost impossible to leave due to the risk of execution. The combat group substituted for lost family and friends.

Child soldiers, most of whom were between the ages of eight and fourteen, became a prominent feature of RUF forces constituting almost one half of all RUF soldiers. In *Fate of Africa*, Martin Meredith reveals that:

> RUF 'town commanders' were given free rein to inflict any punishment they saw fit - hacking off hands and feet became a RUF trademark. Insurgents looted whatever they wanted from the civilian population as their reward. There was no ideology, no political strategy, behind the RUF; only the use of brute force. Hundreds of thousands fled their homes to escape its campaign of terror.
>
> (Martin Meredith, *Fate of Africa*, 2005, p. 564)

Exacerbating the upheaval in these two countries was the formation of yet another militia in September 1991, calling itself The United Liberation Movement for Democracy in Liberia (ULIMO) consisting of the remnants of Doe's army whose main purpose was to rid the country of Taylor.

In 1991, another ECOWAS mediation effort led to an accord calling for disarmament and elections but failed to win over Taylor who continued his objective of capturing the government in Liberia and Sierra Leone.

Taylor's resistance to these offers for an accord was somewhat paradoxical given that he was running into more opposition from ULIMO in the North-west corner of Liberia. ULIMO formed an alliance with ECOMOG forces against Taylor, strengthening the opposition against him.

When Taylor launched yet another attack on Monrovia in October 1992 and bombarded the city with mortar and rocket fire, he came close to capturing ECOMOG's headquarters but ultimately failed when reinforcements were called in. It was at this point that Taylor reluctantly reached the conclusion that he was not capable of taking over all of Liberia by force.

He was now ready to reach a settlement with ECOMOG but two such attempts failed in July 1993 and September 1994 with the various factions continuing to fight each other for dominance. Believing that he could win control of Liberia through negotiations, Taylor continued to talk to ECOMOG for two years before an agreement was reached.

In August 1995, ECOMOG and Taylor reached an accord known as the Abuju Agreement signed by eight faction leaders which called for an interim government run by a Council of State consisting of six members, including Taylor, until elections could be held in August 1996. It also provided for the comprehensive deployment of ECOMOG forces throughout Liberia to monitor a disarmament process.

Finally, after 150,000 lives had been lost during the civil war, Taylor was able to enter Monrovia as a member of the Council of State. As in the past, the peace agreement was short-lived as Krahn and Taylor's forces engaged in a brutal war while ECOMOG forces participated in the looting spree.

By August 1996, all factions were ready again to negotiate and signed Abuju II which provided for the reconstitution of the Council of State and set May 1997 as the date for elections. ECOMOG demanded that the warring factions be dismantled setting January 1997 as the deadline for completion of the process.

ECOMOG warned that this would be the final peace agreement they would underwrite and threatened parties who didn't comply with penalties such as frozen assets and charges of war crimes. At this point, Taylor was satisfied with the agreement due to his success in regaining a considerable amount of territory and the conversion of his militia into a political party for the upcoming elections.

After 16 years of civil war, Liberians went to the polls to elect a new government. Unwilling to trust the voters to elect him president, Taylor used his vast wealth to bribe voters and hire thugs to intimidate voters who refused to be bribed. Although theoretically Taylor had dismantled his militias, he retained sufficient forces to maintain control over 80% of the country where the outcome of the vote would not be in doubt. Another factor influencing voters was the fear that if Taylor did not win the election, he would resort to force again thus dashing any hopes for peace.

Not surprisingly, Taylor won a decisive victory with 75% of the vote, 49 out of 64 seats in the National Assembly and 21 out of 26 seats in the Senate. Thus Taylor finally became the leader of Liberia, perhaps by the only method possible, rigged elections.

United States stake in Liberia in 1996 was to support a leader who would serve American interests notwithstanding his human rights record or the fairness of elections. Since Washington believed Taylor to be that leader, their reaction to the electoral process was very positive. On August 1, 1997, a statement released by the Presidential Press Secretary of the United States referred to the high-powered delegation to Taylor's inauguration as: "representative of the high regard in which we hold the Liberian people for conducting free, peaceful and transparent elections under extremely difficult circumstances." (Office of the Press Secretary, *U.S. Delegation to the Presidential Inauguration in Liberia*, August 1, 1997)

As President, Taylor demonstrated little or no interest in rebuilding Liberia or improving the lives of its people. Both unemployment and illiteracy stalled at 75% throughout his presidency. According to Human Rights Watch:

After five years in office, President Charles Taylor's government continues to function without accountability, exacerbating the divisions and resentments fuelled by the war. Taylor has steadily consolidated and centralised power.(Human Rights Watch, *Back to the Brink: War crimes by the Liberian government and rebels*, New York: 2002)

Despite Taylor's lack of progress economically and socially and his terrible human rights record, President Clinton decided to legitimize his regime through a number of unmistakable gestures. To set their relationship on a sound footing, Clinton designated his close friend Jesse Jackson as a special envoy to Liberia and arranged a meeting between them for February, 1998. The meeting was a success and Taylor could now relax, confident that the United States supported his government.

Two weeks later while Bill Clinton was on his way to a safari, Clinton further boosted Taylor's confidence in continuing U.S. support with a thirty minute conversation through a downlink from Air Force One.

Shortly thereafter, Charles Taylor ordered Foday Sanko and the RUF to return to Sierra Leone where they began an orgy of mass murder. State Department reports describe the slaughter as "brutal killings, severe mutilations and deliberate dismemberments." (U.S. Department of State, *Sierra Leone Country Report on Human Rights Practices for 1998*, February 1999)

Tracing back events on the Sierra Leone front, in 1994, Sankoh and the RUF had won a large proportion of the diamond fields and revenue of $300 million in diamond mine traffic. In addition, he had gained control of the bauxite and titanium mines depriving the government of all its major sources of revenues.

Heading into 1995, Sankoh and the RUF were poised to attack Freetown. To avoid defeat, the president of Sierra Leone, Valentine Strasser, who had seized power in April 1992, hired a private security firm from South Africa, Executive Outcomes, to provide him with the military power he needed to defend Freetown and retake control of the diamond fields lost to Sankoh. He offered to pay them in diamonds in exchange for their successes.

After Executive Outcomes had secured Freetown from Sankoh's forces, they integrated Sierra Leone forces into their own operations after retraining Sierra Leone soldiers..

Despite the fact that most of the country was still rife with civil war, Executive Outcomes had retaken all the diamond mines from Sankoh. Nevertheless, Sankoh continued to wage battle against villages in the North and East of Sierra Leone, part of the purpose of which was to disrupt elections that had been called for in March 1996. Ahmed Tejan Kabbah won the elections as leader of Sierra Leone's People's Party.

Kabbah offered to negotiate a peace agreement with Sankoh without any real success. To bolster his near-bankrupt treasury, Kabbah accepted foreign aid in exchange for terminating the services of Executive Outcomes and other foreign troops.

Continued attacks by RUF forces forced Kabbah to depend on Nigerian forces and international aid to boost his resistance against

Sankoh. He also needed them to weaken opposition forces by arresting army officers supporting a group known as the Armed Forces Revolutionary Council (AFRC). AFRC were a contingent of soldiers from the Sierra Leone army who aligned themselves with the RUF either because they resented the financial neglect by the government, ethnic favoritism or anger at the government for not reaching a peace agreement.

In July 1998, Nigerian soldiers captured Sankoh and shipped him back to Freetown to be tried for treason. RUF forces warned Kabbah that unless he released Sankoh they would launch a crusade of terror against the people of Sierra Leone.

Convicted of treason and sentenced to death in October, 1998, Sankoh waited on death row during his appeals while RUF forces fulfilled their promise by massacring, mutilating and abducting children. In their march toward Freetown, they RUF massacred some 6,000 civilians, amputated hands and feet at random and destroyed buildings and homes.

U.S diplomacy intervened again with Jesse Jackson as the envoy whose mission was to bring about a ceasefire and to persuade Kabbah not to execute Sankoh. According to Jackson, "Kabah had just executed some of Sankoh's guys and was about to execute Sankoh. So we appealed to Kabbah not to kill Sankoh." (Thomas, *The Blood on Jesse Jackson's Hands*, April 16 2007)

Jackson was basically asking the President of Sierra Leone not to execute a barbaric war criminal. The Washington Post claims that:

> Instead of convening a war crimes tribunal for the leaders of this brutal campaign, the United States is backing a peace accord that would put eight of them in the cabinet of the democratically elected government...The United states dispatched Jesse L. Jackson to urge the country's president to come to terms with the rebels. (Steven Mufson, *U.S. Backs Amnesty in Sierra Leone*, Washington Post, October 18, 1999, p. A13)

Conveying the same message, the New Republic states that:

> The peace agreement signed in Lomé, Togo - an agreement that forced the democratic president of Sierra Leone to hand over much of his government and most of his country's wealth to one of the greatest monsters of the late twentieth century - was conceived and implemented by the United States. (Ryan Pizza, *Where Angels Fear to Tread*, The New Republic, July 24, 2000)

After a decade of civil war, the Lomé Peace Accord was signed by all the warring parties on July 7, 1999. President Kabbah and Sankoh both signed the agreement which granted Sankoh the position of vice president in the transitional government. After eight years of chopping off limbs, recruiting children and mass slaughter, the RUF had finally bludgeoned its way to power.

To convince Kabbah to sign an agreement which would offer his arch enemy the office of vice president in addition to four cabinet posts and four deputy posts, Joseph Melrose, U.S. Ambassador to Sierra Leone, shuttled back and forth between Freetown and Lomé, the Capital of Togo.

Convincing Kabbah to attend a peace conference with Sakoh proved to be very challenging. Kabbah was attending an African summit meeting in Accra, Ghana. Jackson pressured Kabbah to attend the meeting with Sankoh and arranged for a helicopter to take him to Lomé. When two of Kabah's aids, who were opposed to any meeting with Sankoh, tried to board the helicopter, Jackson declared that there was no more room.

Once again, the U.S. drew a veil of secrecy over events in Africa covering up their role in installing a barbaric killer as vice president of Sierra Leone. Assistant Secretary of State, Susan Rice testified before the Senate Foreign Relations Committee that Lomé was "a test of our commitment to democracy and human rights in Africa." (Steven Mufson, *U.S. Backs Amnesty in Sierra Leone*, Washington Post, October 18, 1999, p. A13) Peace was short-lived. Sierra Leone remained divided between regions under RUF control and regions under ECOMOG control. RUF's control over the KONO diamond fields financed continuance of the war, enabling them to increase their control over Sierra Leone.

It wasn't until the United Nations intervened that a real peace and disarmament process was introduced. Originally, the United Nation's had authorized a peace-keeping mission in June 1998 known as the United Nations Observer Mission in Sierra Leone (UNOMISL) to monitor and advise efforts to disarm combatants and to restructure the nation's security forces.

Due to its inadequate resources, UNOMISL was unable to achieve its objectives and was replaced by the United Nations Mission in Sierra Leone (UNAMISL) on October 2, 1999 with 6,000 military personnel to assist the parties in carrying out the terms of the Lomé Agreement.

Its maiden efforts in Sierra Leone nearly collapsed when the RUF kidnapped hundreds of peacekeepers and renounced the ceasefire. Foreign powers applied pressure on the RUF to comply with the terms of the ceasefire and imposed sanctions against all RUF sponsors.

Despite RUF's attempt to disrupt the peace process, UNAMISL was able to restart it, assisted by an increase in UN troops to 11,100 on February 7, 2000, then to 13,000 on May 19, 2000 and finally to 17,500 on March 30, 2001.

Britain had also intervened in May 2000 with a fully armed expeditionary force to prevent Freetown from being overrun by RUF forces. Sankoh was forced to escape but was captured ten days later. After he was captured, he was handed over to the Sierra Leone government despite pleas by Taylor that he be sent to a third country. Following the arrest of Sankoh, the RUF fragmented into small groups and lost their momentum.

Britain concentrated on restructuring the army while UNAMISL trained the local police force and focused on ending the illicit trade in diamonds which had financed rebel groups during the conflict.

By the time peace had prevailed, 50,000 people had died, 20,000 were mutilated and three-quarters of the population had been displaced.

The United Nations mission had been very successful in Sierra Leone counting among its achievements disarming 75,490 combatants, 55,000 ex-fighters receiving reintegration benefits, collecting 42,330 weapons and 1.2 million rounds of ammunition from combatants. A majority of the 6,800 demobilized children were reunited with their families. (UN, *Sierra Leone-UNAMISL*, Peace and Security Section of Public Relations, 2009)

On May 14, 2002, general elections were held in Sierra Leone to elect a president and parliament. Kabah was elected president with 70% of the vote.

Weaknesses in the whole electoral process from voter registration to counting of votes were well documented by the Carter Centre. Some of their criticisms include shortage of time for proper preparation, high illiteracy rate, inadequate staff at registration centres and lack of media and voter education. (Carter Centre, *The Democracy Program*, May 2003)

Predictably, many concerns lingered after the election. Tensions between the Temme in the North who were underrepresented in parliament and the Mende in the South and central part of the country, who were vastly overrepresented, were cause for concern that Kabbah and his party, Sierra Leone's People's Party (SLPP), constituted a one-party system. As well, Kabbah had the immense challenge of eradicating the deeply-rooted corruption system that prevailed throughout the country. In addition, there were many disgruntled soldiers and disenfranchised youth wandering the streets of Freetown.

Donor country's' concern about corruption led them to assist in developing control mechanisms within the Ministry of Finance. However, they became frustrated with the slow progress in eliminating corruption.

One positive reform implemented by Kabbah was to initiate local government reform and decentralize programs for the purpose of improving the structures of government at the local level.

Progressing to the next level, Sierra Leone held elections in 2007 ushering in a new president, Ernest Bai Koroma of the All People's Congress (APC), and vice-president, Solomon Berewa of the SLPP.

The National Democratic Institute was invited to monitor and evaluate the election. They reported that:

> Sierra Leone's 2007 presidential election and legislative elections offered citizens an opportunity to consolidate the gains made since the end of the armed conflict in 2002 by providing genuine competition for political power at both the presidential and parliamentary levels. The peaceful conduct of Sierra Leone's election bodes well for the country's future stability and development. (National Democratic Institute, *NDI's Final Report on Sierra Leone's 2007 Elections*, 2008)

November 17, 2012, marked the third set of elections since the conflict ended in 2002. Ernest Bai Koroma won the presidency with 58% of the vote. Ban Ki Moon, Secretary-general of the United Nations, congratulated the people of Sierra Leone for holding a fair and open election.

After so much suffering and terror, the people of Sierra Leone are not only free from the sinister influence of the RUF but also from the malevolent Charles Taylor who supported the RUF for so many years.

Most of the diamonds mined in Sierra Leone during the years of conflict were smuggled through Liberia and handled by traders acting on Taylor's behalf. While the RUF and Sanko were enjoying successes in Sierra Leone's gold fields, Taylor was able to enhance his own fortune.

As well as interfering in the affairs of Sierra Leone, Taylor became involved in other regional rebellions hoping to benefit from them as well. For example, he sponsored a rebel group in Guinea by providing it with bases in northern Liberia for the purpose of overthrowing President Lansana Conté.

Taylor's encroachment into Guinea backfired when Conté began supporting Liberian dissidents aiming to overthrow Taylor. In 1999, a new rebel group, calling itself Liberians United for Reconciliation and Democracy (LURD) consisting of anti-Taylor factions, gained a foothold in Lofa county in April, 2000, in north-west Liberia using Guinea as a rear base of operations. Its mission was to remove Taylor from power.

LURD continued to gain control of counties in north-west Liberia with its headquarters at Tubmanburg in Bomi County.

In March 2003, a second rebel group was formed called the Movement for Democracy and Elections in Liberia (MODEL) which gained control of the south and east of Liberia.

LURD rapidly advanced toward Monrovia looting, raping and abducting children en route. On June 4, 2003, LURD mounted an attack on Monrovia in a series of bloody battles but it ultimately failed to capture the capital. The shelling of the city resulted in the death of 1,000 civilians and the displacement of tens of thousands of people.

In addition to the warfare waged by LURD and MODEL, external pressures from a West African peacekeeping force headed by Nigeria known as the Economic Community of West African States (ECOMIL) joined with UN peacekeepers and in conjunction with pressures from the international community eventually forced Taylor to reach the inevitable conclusion that he had to resign.

On August 11, 2003, Taylor relinquished power, unburdening the people of Liberia and surrounding countries of this predatory monster whose only mission in life was self-aggrandizement and power at all costs.

The Liberian government, rebels, political parties and leaders from civil society signed a peace agreement in Accra on August 18, 2003, that laid the framework for a two-year national transitional government of Liberia (NTGL) under the presidency of businessman Gyude Bryant. The NTGL was to function as a transitional government until elections scheduled for October 2005.

One of Bryant's decisions while head of the transitional government was to extend the land concession granted to Firestone for a further 36 years as part of his efforts to revive the economy after 14 years of civil war. By extending the concession without any conditions, he was perpetuating the extreme human rights violations on the plantation, consisting of child labor and adult forced labor. Some of the workers were working up to 21 hours a day in order to meet their quotas.

In November 2005, The International Labor Rights Fund (ILRF) filed an Alien Torts Claims Act case in US District Court in California against the rubber company alleging "forced labor, the modern equivalent of slavery". ILRF executive director, Terry Collingsworth, filed the suit on behalf of 12 Liberian workers and their 23 children. Bridgestone defeated the class certification of Alien Tort Claims Act charges of forced labor on its Liberian plantation on March 4, 2009.

On a more positive note, the Security Council adopted resolution 1509 establishing the UN Mission in Liberia (UNMIL) and calling for the deployment of 15,000 UN peacekeeping troops to establish stability and order. Part of its mission was to undertake a voluntary disarmament program, collect and destroy weapons and to provide security for key government installations and infrastructure.

Peace still seemed elusive as the tensions between different factions did not easily dissipate and disarmament proved to be a difficult undertaking. On the other hand, by the end of 2004, UNMIL had disarmed 100,000 soldiers. As well as disarming the fighters, UNMIL also developed a program to reintegrate the soldiers back into society.

With UNMIL safeguarding the peace, the transitional government proceeded with the task of preparing the country for fair and peaceful democratic elections to be held on October 11, 2005.

Ellen Johnson Sirleaf won the election and became the first women president of an African country. She was a Harvard-trained economist who had served as an economist at the World Bank.

She was successfully in securing forgiveness of billions of dollars of Liberia's debt and in transforming Liberia's image of a war-torn, brutal country to one of a stable country with a progressive government. In recognition of her accomplishments in Liberia, she was jointly awarded the Nobel Peace Prize in October 2011. On November 10, 2011, she won a second term as president.

Liberia is another tragic example of the United States ignoring human rights and brutal, corrupt dictators to serve its own interests. Whomever the United States deemed to be an American-friendly leader was supported in power, notwithstanding their human rights record or the type of government they established. On the other hand, leaders who defied, challenged or simply became too much of an embarrassment were undermined by the U.S. Underlying the political intervention was the promotion of American economic interests and corporate profits.

Post-colonialism manifested itself in the crusade to maintain control over a country for the purpose of exploitation. It is a transmuted extension of colonialism in the sense that the dominant country eschews direct rule in favor of control through its vast military or economic superiority in order to impose rapacious exploitation.

By supporting a friendly dictator who acts as a surrogate American imperator, control is maintained to almost the same extent as in colonial times. The pitfall in such a relationship between surrogate and dominant country is that a dictator can be unpredictable and not always perform according to the prescriptions of the master. On the other hand, the master enjoys the option of replacing one puppet with another thus restoring complete control.

When a country's government is democratic in nature, the challenge of gaining control is formidable due to the fact that the elected members of the government are at least nominally beholden to the people whereas a dictator often can be bribed or pressured into serving the interests of the dominant country. When such an obstacle arises, the solution is often the overthrow of the democratic government as in the Congo.

World Systems Theory does not quite capture the degree of political control on which imperialism depends for its rapacious exploitation. World Systems Theory defines a natural order of economic relations between resource-based developing countries and industrialized developed countries while imperialism can be much more brutal in nature when the dominant country installs or supports an unpopular dictator using force as the means to remain in control for the purpose of exploitation.

In Africa, imperialism was the nature of exploitation and human rights, international law and morality were sacrificed on the altar of avarice.